Something must be

Known and Felt

*A missing note in
today's Christianity*

Stuart Olyott

Evangelical Movement of Wales

The EMW works in both Welsh and English and seeks to help Christians and churches by:
- running children's camps and family conferences
- providing theological training and events for ministers
- running Christian bookshops and a conference centre
- publishing magazines and books

Bryntirion Press is a ministry of EMW

Past issues of EMW magazines and sermons preached at our conferences are available on our web site: www.emw.org.uk

Published by

Bryntirion Press, Evangelical Movement of Wales, Waterton Cross Business Park, South Road, Bridgend, CF31 3UL

Bryntirion Press, Mudiad Efengylaidd Cymru, Waterton Cross Business Park, South Road, Pen-y-Bont ar Ogwr, CF31 3UL

In association with EP BOOKS, Faverdale North, Darlington, DL3 0PH, UK.

EP BOOKS are distributed in the USA by:
JPL Fulfillment, 3741 Linden Avenue Southeast, Grand Rapids, MI 49548.
E-mail: sales@jplfulfillment.com
Tel: 877.683.6935

Printed and bound in the UK by 4edge Limited

Contents

Introduction: Why this book?

True religion's more than notion;
Something must be known and felt.
JOSEPH HART (1712–68)[1]

This is a book about the place of feelings in the Christian life and about some aspects of spiritual experience. I have written it because, right now, such a book is needed.

The gospel continues to spread on every continent and we are filled with daily thanks for what the Lord is doing in countless lives everywhere. This said, modern Evangelicalism, especially in the West, is often very different from the religion of the Bible.

Today's Christianity is largely composed of doctrine (believing the right things), ethics (behaving in the right way) and methodology (doing church and evangelism in the best possible way). It is a three-legged stool, but it is not the same shape as the three-legged stool of God's Word. There we find that methodology is not of any great importance.

The three legs on which biblical religion stands are doctrine, ethics and *experience*—God's revealed truth is believed, it is lived out, and it is *felt*. It impacts the soul. If we forget this we will eventually lose biblical religion altogether.

Some early personal history

I suppose I am a bit surprised to find myself writing about all this. I was brought up in a family where feelings were profound, but any expression of them was discouraged. I and my brothers knew that our parents loved us greatly, but we seldom, if ever, heard them telling us so. When my brother Stephen died at the age of forty-seven, I knew that my widowed mother was heartbroken, because she said, 'Oh dear'. This, for her, was the cry of an agonised heart.

As a result of such an upbringing, I and my remaining brothers still find it hard to talk about what we feel. Some people have therefore concluded that we don't have any feelings at all! Nothing could be further from the truth. 'Still waters run deep' is certainly true of us.

My conversion to Christ in my mid-teens was a time of soul-shaking emotion. For a year or more I was distressed by my sin and by the consciousness that I wasn't saved. This was so upsetting to me, and the ungodly pressures from my closest friends were so strong, that I ended up with one strong desire—to get away from my Christian parents and all other gospel influences, so as to be like everyone else. I saw my chance of making the break when, one weekend in the autumn of 1957, I went to stay with my paternal grandmother in Colchester, Essex.

On the Sunday morning my grandmother did not make me go to church and I felt as free as a bird. But things changed in the afternoon. Somehow, in a way that I cannot fully explain, I felt hungry inside. I felt that I needed to be where the Bible was opened. But I was afraid of being converted, so I went to a church where it seemed unlikely that gospel truth would be pressed on me in any compelling manner. The minister of the church, whom I knew quite well, duly took the service and then, to my surprise, announced that he was not going to preach. A friend of his, with a life-transforming story to tell, would be preaching instead!

As the unknown man told his story and preached the gospel, I was overcome with a great sense of God, of sin, of judgment, of lostness and of total bewilderment. What a sense of relief I had when he told us about God's willingness to save us! I understood that salvation was somehow tied up with Christ's death on the cross, but could not have explained at the time how this could be so. I knew and felt that I must come to Christ, and there in the back pew of the gallery I cried out to him to have mercy on me. I left the meeting trembling all over and hoping against hope that He had heard my prayer.

Back home in Chester I no longer had any hankering to distance myself from the things of God, but my experience in Colchester had been so traumatic that I was in a state of fear every time I heard a sermon. I was terrified that I might have to go through a similar experience again! Little by little, however, this fear left me, and I began to enjoy increasing comfort in the things of God. At this stage I left my parents' church and joined a small church a mile away which was filled with happy and holy people, many of whom were as young as I was. There I was baptised, became a member, and began to live the Christian life in earnest.

In that church, which had no pastor, I learned to love the Lord, to love His Word, to love His Day, to love His people and to love working for Him. However, despite this surge of love, the emphasis in the church was that feelings were of no importance in the Christian life. In fact the church, with all its wonderful qualities, was an enigma. We sang choruses like, 'In my heart there rings a melody', 'I've got the joy, joy, joy, joy down in my heart' and 'Sweeter as the days go by', and yet were told again and again that our feelings did not matter! I felt the melody, knew the joy, found the days sweeter, but found myself trotting out the accepted line that belief and behaviour were the only vitally important dimensions of the Christian life.

Hywel Griffiths

This is the way it remained until, as a family, we moved to the village of Cosheston in West Wales, by which time I was a theological student. There, in the village's chapel, I had the life-changing privilege of sitting under the ministry of the Rev. Hywel Griffiths, who had come to preach for a week of special meetings. In a damp building without electricity, hidden away at the end of a short lane, the Lord dealt with me in a way that would direct the whole of my future thinking, behaviour and ministry.

Hywel Griffiths, minister of Litchard Mission Church, Bridgend, had been converted during his time as a coal miner, and had been wonderfully helped by the Rev. R. B. Jones, who had given him a great deal of his time and attention. By the time he came to Cosheston Hywel was in his mid-sixties and had been in the ministry for about twenty-five years. He had first come to the village a year earlier, and my mother had urged me to come away from my theological studies for a few days so that I could hear him—which, regrettably, I was not able to do. She said that there was something about Hywel that could not be put into words. She told me that I would understand if I could hear him for myself. All she could tell me was that it was wonderful.

It was more than that, as I found out a year later. Hywel Griffiths preached lengthily, filled his sermons with word pictures, clearly felt in his soul the truths he was proclaiming, and poured out his love for everyone present. Accompanying all that was an indefinable influence. As Hywel spoke, heaven came to earth. Another Voice was heard. The invisible world was more real than the visible one. There was a touch of glory. Christ was more precious than anything or anyone in the universe. The Word came over with a self-authenticating force that was irresistible. Not to believe was not an option, because it was indescribably foolish. The only wise thing to do was to trust the Lord completely, and to love Him with all of my heart, soul, mind and strength.

You must not think that I was alone in receiving these impressions. After each sermon the congregation sat in stunned silence, overcome by the sheer power of the Word. Sometimes the silence was followed by spontaneous prayer, where one and another cried out to the Lord, wept their way to the cross, or renewed their vows to love Him and to live for Him. And I, like many others, was changed for ever. We had experienced a small taste of what happens in revival. We all knew now that there was such a thing as preaching with 'unction',[2] and that there were panoramas of spiritual understanding and paths of spiritual experience of which we knew virtually nothing. Nothing had happened to diminish our belief in the importance of doctrine and ethics, but they, on their own, would never satisfy us again. We would now rather die than have a religion without a felt Christ.

From then until now

It is now over fifty years since those wonderful days in Cosheston. What Hywel taught us is still remembered and valued there, although he would hardly recognise the chapel (now called Cosheston Mission Church) today. The lane has been surfaced and there is a car park at the end. The building has been extended to include a schoolroom, study, kitchen and toilets. It has a damp course, electricity, heating and double glazing. Everything, it seems, has improved. But, in Evangelicalism as a whole, things have hardly improved at all. If it were possible, Cosheston would gladly welcome Hywel back, as would dozens of other churches. But, frankly, I don't believe that the vast majority of Evangelicals in today's world would be interested in a ministry like his. Their minds are elsewhere, and they are the poorer for it.

Nonetheless, felt Christianity with a supernatural touch has not entirely gone from the earth, and we must do what we can to help believers know about it, to seek it, and to not be satisfied with anything less.

This will not be easy. It is likely that people will believe that we consider ourselves to be members of a spiritual elite, when in fact all we are is humbly grateful for the way that the Lord has taken us. Others will write us off as touchy-feely fanatics. Yet others will accuse us of no longer having the Bible as our sole authority for all matters of faith and practice, and of having our feelings as a second authority. It doesn't matter what people may say. Biblical Christianity the world over is in danger of being permanently deformed, and we must do something about it, whatever it may cost us personally.

Believers need to know that 'without powerful, personal dealings between a man and his God, religion is a sham'.[3] They need to know that feelings are part and parcel of a true Christian's experience, and how to tell the difference between holy emotions and unspiritual ones. They need to know something of how the Holy Spirit works in the soul. They need to know that it is possible to feel that you are a child of God and to have the experience of being guided by Him. They need to know about the felt presence of Christ and how to distinguish it from its counterfeits. They need to know about the prayer of faith—I think it is safe to conclude that most believers today have never heard of such a thing. They need to know what it is to have a 'heart strangely warmed',[4] and why the heart really is at the centre of all true religion.

These are the subjects that this book will touch on, and it will do so in as biblical a manner as possible. But I do not want anyone to think that I am writing of things beyond my experience. I am well aware of my many failings in my walk with the Lord and of my constant need to be cleansed in the blood of Christ. Yet I know what it is to have holy feelings—feelings which are so deep that I have literally been dumbfounded in prayer, or so affected by God's truth that it has been impossible to speak to anyone after preaching a sermon. I know what it is to have the Holy Spirit stir my soul. I both know and feel myself to be in God's family. I have felt the presence of the risen Christ. I know what it is to be guided by God. In prayer, and after it, I have often known the outcome of an event yet to take place. Waiting on the Lord has been the joy of my life. And there is a fire in my heart even now as I write these words.

I have no doubt that there are many who could write more competently on all of these subjects but, at the moment, there are very few who are doing it. So, child that I am, I am offering to the Lord my five loaves and two fish and am asking Him to bless them. My hope is that they will be multiplied, distributed widely, and used by the Master to feed men and women who have hungry souls. Lord, hear my prayer!

STUART OLYOTT
Connah's Quay, North Wales,
September 2014

1. Emotions in the Bible

*I preached what I felt, what I smartingly
did feel ... I preached what I saw and felt.*

JOHN BUNYAN[5]

The Bible has to a lot to say about our emotions and its teaching needs to be clear to us, especially as there is so much confusion about this subject. As I have already told you, in my early Christian life I was left with the impression that our feelings didn't matter. There are still lots of well-meaning people today who teach the same thing. Other Christian circles, however, seem to be saying that our feelings matter more than anything else. In addition to these contradictory voices, we have more and more people coming into our churches who have emotional problems. And which one of us will dare to say that we have no such problems ourselves?

I want this book to be reasonably short—otherwise no one will read it! This means that we cannot study this question in the depth that it deserves. Even so, this chapter will still be one of the longest in the book. This is because we need to build everything on a solid Scriptural foundation, which is something we can't do in a hurry. Nor can we do it without sometimes sounding a bit technical.

As we study this subject in the light of God's Word, it seems to me that there are six main points for us to grasp. These six points make up the six sections of this chapter.[6]

1. Our nature as men and women: we are body and soul

We must start by enquiring about our human make-up. We humans, what are we? We are, first of all, body. When God created our ancestor Adam, it is said that 'The Lord God formed man of the dust of the ground' (Genesis 2:7). The human body, in and of itself, is good—having a body is not a reason to be ashamed! It is not the seat of sin, because human bodies existed before sin came into the world. Nor was the body originally mortal; it only became so as a result of the Fall. It is important for me to recognise that my body is as much *me* as any other part of me. What is laid in the grave at death is not without value. It is not just a thing. It is the *person* as respects the body, 'for dust *you* are, and to dust *you* shall return' (Genesis 3:19).

Not only so, but we are also spirit (or soul). There is an aspect of our life and existence which is to be distinguished from the body—something that has qualities which prevent it from undergoing the disintegration and destruction that happen to the body after death. The Scriptures call this *spirit* or *soul*.

This is why we read of our Lord saying such things as, 'Do not fear those who kill the body but cannot kill the soul'

(Matthew 10:28) and, 'The spirit indeed is willing, but the flesh is weak' (Matthew 26:41). This is why the Scriptures record our Lord's death on the cross by saying that 'bowing his head, he gave up his spirit' (John 19:30). In the same way, when Stephen's dying body was being stoned, he prayed, 'Lord Jesus, receive my spirit' (Acts 7:59).

There are, then, two aspects to our being; we are spirit (or soul), as well as body. There are two entities in our constitution. One, our body, is derived from the earth—it is material (made up of matter), corporeal (made up of organs which depend on each other), phenomenal (perceived by the senses, rather than the mind) and divisible (you can chop it up into pieces). The other, our spirit, is derived from a distinct action of God. It is immaterial (there is no matter in its make-up), ordinarily not phenomenal (you can't normally detect it with the senses), indivisible (it can't be chopped into pieces) and indestructible (it can never be destroyed).

These two, body and spirit, form one organic unit, namely *me*! As I was once told as a boy, each one of us is 'a psychosomatic unity'! I have never forgotten what I was told, but at that time I couldn't understand what was being said. It means, quite simply, that I am body and I am soul, but that there is only one *me*. But body and soul are inter-dependent—the state of my body affects the state of my soul; and the state of my soul affects the state of my body. Body and soul co-act and interact in a way which is impossible for us to finally analyse; the union between them is intimate and intricate.

I am well aware, of course, that some people teach that there are not two aspects to our existence, but three—namely body, soul and spirit. Such people tell us that soul and spirit are not the same thing. The fact is, however, that the Bible does not make a hard and fast distinction between the two, nor are we conscious ourselves of such a distinction. Yes, it is true that the Hebrew Old Testament and the Greek New Testament use two different words for soul and spirit, but this does not mean that they are talking about different things. The word *soul* sometimes refers to man in his entirety, but is more often used to distinguish the immaterial part of me from the material part of me. The soul is what makes me alive. The word *spirit* is most often used to talk about my human personality before God. It is also used to refer to my rationality, that is, my ability to reason. The two words emphasise different aspects of the hidden part of me, but are not intended to tell me that I am a threesome. No; I am body and soul (spirit) and no more.

2. Emotions have their root in the human soul (spirit)

The soul does not have hands and feet, and the body does not have emotions. Emotions have their root in the soul. We can easily illustrate this by quoting some Bible verses which speak about two of our most common emotions, sorrow and joy:

Sorrow

'Why are you cast down, O my soul?' (Psalm 42:5).

'O my God, my soul is cast down within me' (Psalm 42:6).

'The Lord is near to those who have a broken heart, and saves such as have a contrite spirit' (Psalm 34:18).

'Now my soul is troubled' (John 12:27).

'My soul is exceedingly sorrowful, even to death'
(Matthew 26:38).

'Now while Paul waited for them at Athens, his spirit was
provoked within him when he saw that the city was
given over to idols' (Acts 17:16).

'For that righteous man, dwelling among them, tormented
his righteous soul from day to day by seeing and
hearing their lawless deeds' (2 Peter 2:8).

Joy

'My soul shall be satisfied as with marrow and fatness, and
my mouth shall praise you with joyful lips' (Psalm 63:5).

'Return to your rest, O my soul, for the Lord has dealt
bountifully with you' (Psalm 116:7).

'My soul magnifies the Lord, and my spirit has rejoiced in
God my Saviour' (Luke 1:46–47).

'For they refreshed my spirit and yours'
(1 Corinthians 16:18).

'We rejoiced exceedingly more for the joy of Titus, because his
spirit has been refreshed by you all' (2 Corinthians 7:13).

'We ... have strong consolation, who have fled for refuge to
lay hold of the hope set before us. This hope we have as
an anchor of the soul' (Hebrews 6:18–19).

So, then, each one of us is body and soul, but our emotions
have their root only in the soul. This does not mean that they

are unaffected by the state of our body because, as we have seen, body and soul interact in a way which none of us can understand or define. It is important for us to remember this for it explains, among other things, why certain medications administered to the body can affect, and even alter, the emotions.

3. The human soul has two parts

When we probe more deeply what the Bible has to say about the soul, we discover that it teaches us that the soul has two parts. Actually, I am not sure that we should really use the word 'parts' at all, but it is hard to find another satisfactory word. The fact is that the soul is indivisible. It cannot be divided into two 'bits'. Its 'parts' are not as clearly different to each other as are body and soul. As long as this is clear, the word 'parts' will do for now. And the two parts of the soul are *the understanding* (or intellect) and *the will*.

This has always been the belief of historic biblical Protestantism. So it is that John Calvin writes: 'The human soul has two parts, the understanding and the will. It is the province of the understanding to discern between good and evil, and of the will to make its choice between the two.'[7]

a) The understanding

Let us talk first about *the understanding*, which we could also call our intellect, our mind or our thought life. Thinking and understanding are clearly activities of the soul. For example, in 1 Corinthians 2:11 the apostle Paul asks the question, 'For what man knows the things of a man except the spirit of the man which is in him?' Whatever may be the place of the brain, knowing things is an activity of the spirit and not of the body. It thinks thoughts which are known to itself, but which are completely unknown to everybody else. If I were in the same room as you, you would not know what I was thinking unless I told you.

But we don't just think thoughts. We examine and evaluate things. We weigh them up. So we are not indifferent to what we are thinking about. We are not just spectators who watch events but remain unaffected by them. We like things or dislike them. We are pleased or displeased by them. We approve them or reject them. Sometimes we call this second faculty our *inclination*, but when we talk about in relation to the decisions that we make we usually call it *the will*.

b) The will

How does the human will operate? We either move towards the things we see, by liking or approving them, or we turn away from them and reject them. Sometimes the movement is hardly detectable—our inclination is so slight that it is almost total apathy. On other occasions we are strongly drawn towards something, or utterly revolted by it.

Our forefathers called these energetic and intense acts of the will 'the affections', and I personally think that this is a good word to use. Today, however, when we are similarly moved towards or away from something, we mostly use the word 'emotions'. It is the experience of being moved. It is a strong *motion* of the will.

The Bible is clear: the soul is not composed of three elements (the mind, the emotions and the will) but only of two (the mind and the will). Our will and our emotions are not two separate things. When the inclination/will is strongly attracted or strongly repulsed, when it is moved for or against, we call it 'an emotion'. But when the same faculty works in the same way, but with less intensity, we tend to call it 'a simple choice'. But there is not a difference of kind between these two experiences. There is only a difference of intensity.

Emotions are strong movements of the will

This will become clearer if we give some examples. If we saw a child killed before our eyes, we would be shocked and horrified. Something inside us would cry out, 'No! No! No!' But if we saw a child in extreme danger wonderfully rescued, we would be thrilled. Something inside us would cry out, 'Yes! Yes! Yes!' The inward 'No!' and 'Yes!' are strong movements of the will. Such movements are what we call *emotion*.

But if I put before you a green apple and a red one, and then asked you to choose one, you would probably not be very bothered about which one to pick. However, you would eventually say 'Yes' to one, and therefore 'No' to the other. It would still be a movement of the will, but not a strong one. Such a simple choice we tend to call *inclination*.

This sort of reasoning may not be interesting you very much, so let us get back to the Bible. The Word of God clearly teaches that the emotions are part and parcel of the volition, that is, the will. We will all admit that fear is an emotion. But the Bible's most repeated command is to 'Fear not'. It is an emotion that we are to choose not to have. We are to say 'No' to it. God instructs us to decide against it. Such a command would be nonsense if the emotions were not connected to the will.

When Our Lord is asked to define the greatest commandment of all, He replies that it is the commandment to 'love the Lord your God with all your heart, with all your soul, and with all your mind.' He goes on to say that the second greatest commandment is, 'You shall love your neighbour as yourself.' He then concludes, 'On these two commandments hang all the Law and Prophets.' (Matthew 22:37–40). Love is certainly an emotion. It is saying 'Yes!' to someone, and 'Yes!' to the idea of living for their benefit. The whole of God's revelation in Scripture is telling us to say that 'Yes!'. To say that we are commanded to have an emotion, and to say that we are commanded to have strong movement of the will, is to say the same thing.

Biblical examples

Here are some other Bible verses that show to us that emotions are all tied up with the will:

'Love is the fulfilment of the law' (Romans 13:10).

'Be glad in the Lord and rejoice, you righteous, and shout for joy, all you upright in heart' (Psalm 32:11).

'Rejoice and be exceedingly glad, for great is your reward in heaven' (Matthew 5:12).

'Rejoice in the Lord always. Again I will say, rejoice!' (Philippians 4:4).

'Rejoice always' (1 Thessalonians 5:16).

'Conduct yourselves throughout the time of your
sojourning here in fear' (1 Peter 1:17).

'Fear God and give glory to him' (Revelation 14:7).

Yes, emotions are not distinct from the human will, but intense expressions of it. A strong liking for something is called *love*, while an equally strong dislike is called *hatred*. When we approve strongly of something, the great pleasure we get at that moment is called *joy*; but when we strongly disapprove of something, the displeasure we experience is called *sorrow*.

Every emotion has an opposite

What we call 'emotions', then, are 'affections', and they are not separable from our inclinations or will. This is why every emotion has an opposite, because every emotion is either our moving towards something with an inward 'Yes!', or our moving away from something with an inward 'No!' As we have seen, the opposite of love is hate. The opposite of joy is sorrow. In the same way desire is the opposite of fear, gratitude the opposite of anger, and pleasure the opposite of grief.

Not only does every emotion have an opposite, but it is also possible to have several emotions, even conflicting emotions, at the same time. Most people today, including many Christians, seem unable to grasp this. As far as they are concerned, if you are happy you can't be sad; and love and hate can't possibly be found in the same person at the same time. But their own observation should teach them otherwise. For example, a mother can in the same moment be furiously angry with a child because of its disobedience and yet fiercely protective of it because of her love. A believer can hate the way unconverted people behave while simultaneously loving every person they meet and yearning for their salvation. The human soul can say both a strong 'Yes!' and an equally strong 'No!' at the same time. In fact, being 'sorrowful, yet always rejoicing' (2 Corinthians 6:10) is our condition every day.

4. Genuine spiritual experience is largely a matter of the emotions

We now come to the most important point of this chapter and to the truth to which everything so far has been leading. It is this: genuine spiritual experience is largely a matter of the emotions. No work of God is going on where men and women, boys and girls, are not strongly moved—moved in their inmost being away from something ungodly, and moved in their souls towards God and godliness. Where people have only dull, lifeless wishes, which raise them only a little above apathy, who will dare to say that *God* is at work?

True religion consists in being 'fervent in spirit, serving the Lord; rejoicing in hope' (Romans 12:11–12). It means obeying commandments like: 'Hear, O Israel: The Lord our God, the Lord is one! You shall love the Lord your God with all your heart, with all your soul, and with all your might' (Deuteronomy 6:4–5), and 'Now Israel, what does the Lord require of you, but to fear the Lord your God, to walk in all his ways and to love him ...' (Deuteronomy 10:12).

Some people have a form of godliness, but deny its power (see 2 Timothy 3:5). They know what outward religion is, but know nothing of a religion which springs from the heart and which gives them a spirit 'of power and of love and of a sound mind' (2 Timothy 1:7). They may have read that Christ baptises all who belong to Him with the Holy Spirit and fire (Matthew 3:11), but know nothing of this in their own personal experience.

There is no doubt about it: biblical religion is all about emotion—it is about fear, hope, joy, sorrow, gratitude and zeal. The fruit of the Spirit is love, joy and peace (Galatians 5:22). The essence and core of genuine spiritual experience is love, without which the greatest knowledge, the most extraordinary gifts and all worthy actions are nothing (see 1 Corinthians chapter 13).

Emotions are the lifeblood of Old Testament religion and run through every part of it. The proof of this is the Book of Psalms, where you can find every emotion that a believer can possibly have. In the same way, emotions are found everywhere in the New Testament. Consider the incarnate Son of God, with His love, compassion, joy, disappointment, surprise, anger, sorrow and anguish. Look at Paul, with his joy, tears, hope, godly jealousy, continual sorrow and abounding love. Or listen to the apostle John as he writes about love, love and more love. Throughout the Bible emotions charge every genuine spiritual activity. There is no such thing as an unfelt sermon, either by preacher or listener. Prayers without emotion are not prayers at all. Many prayers are in fact songs—and what is a song except a means of giving expression to the deepest feelings of the heart?

Lack of godly emotion—called 'hardness of heart'—is condemned everywhere in God's Book. The atmosphere of heaven will be one of emotion; it will be a place of joy, of thankfulness, of praise and of love. Any religious expression that is short of these emotions can be neither a foretaste of heaven nor a preparation for it. We must face the facts: clinical, unfeeling Christianity is not authentic Christianity and is a great evil; the wonder is that such large sections of the professing church of Jesus Christ seem to have encouraged it!

We should set a high store on preachers, on prayers, on hymns and on books that *move* us, that affect us deeply, and that reach our hearts. We should be ashamed of how little moved the people in our churches are. Their love is cold. Their spiritual desires are sluggish. Their gratitude is small. In fact, they seem rather bored by everything that is going on.

Week after week goes by, during which we preach about the being and glory of God and His infinite love for us seen in our Lord Jesus Christ. We speak about the Saviour's awful death for us sinners, and the triumph of His resurrection. We teach about the benefits of salvation, now, at our death, and the resurrection, and the last judgement and in eternity. And throughout all this the people in front of us are unmoved—and sometimes we are not moved by it ourselves! Surely this is not New Testament Christianity!

No! Authentic spiritual experience is largely a matter of the emotions. This being so, we are forced to the sad conclusion that there is very, very little genuine spiritual experience around at the moment.

5. This said, we need to stress that there are emotions which are legitimate and emotions which are not

Genuine spiritual experience is largely a matter of the emotions. But this does not mean that all emotions are legitimate. Some are, and some are not. So how are we to know which are which?

Let us put things this way. We want the people in our churches to be people who think, but this does not mean that we want them to have any old thoughts, because it is a fact that some thoughts are displeasing to God. We also want them to be men and women of action, but not just any action, because some actions are displeasing to God. In the same way, we want them to be filled with emotion, but we want them to be spared from having certain emotions, because there are emotions which are not pleasing to God.

However, let us not just talk about others; let us talk about ourselves. How do we decide what is a legitimate thought or action? We measure it against something *outside of itself*, namely the character of God as revealed to us in the Scriptures. We use the same measure in deciding what is a legitimate emotion and what is not.

Sometimes this is easy. For example, if we get pleasure out of seeing others suffer; if we are sad that a friend has been to converted to Christ; if we are happy that we have succeeded where others have failed—it is clear to us that all three of these emotions are illegitimate. This is because they are not in line with the character of God. He has no pleasure in seeing people suffer. He is delighted when anybody is converted. He is the enemy of pride and self-seeking.

But sometimes it is not as straightforward as that. Let us go to a church service where everybody is singing the hymns with gusto. The whole congregation is getting carried away by the beauty, enthusiasm and volume of their music. They are having a sense of occasion, just like they would at an important national event, or at a football or rugby match. But are all these people experiencing emotions which are legitimate?

Let us go to another service, or to a great Christian convention, where a gifted man of God is preaching on sin. Throughout the congregation there are people in distress, many of whom are weeping openly. Then the preacher moves on to speak about assurance of salvation. He explains to his hearers how wonderful it is to be a child of God and to know that that is what you are. At this point, in addition to the weepers, there are countless people beaming with pleasure. But does the Lord approve of all the emotions being expressed? Is He pleased with them all?

Or how about a group of professing Christians who have been out on a day's walk together? As they return to the place where they left their cars you can see that they are all tired and happy. They all report that they have had a great time together. They are all impatient to meet up again soon so that they can enjoy another adventure in each other's company. But are all these people's emotions legitimate?

Legitimate emotions

The answer to these questions is this: *only those emotions are legitimate which maintain the integrity of the person in the sight of God.* This sounds like quite a complicated answer, so what do I mean?

'Integrity' is not a word which we use every day. When most people use it, they take it to mean 'honest' or 'reliable'. But there is more to it than that. Let us think of the word 'disintegrate', which everybody understands. If an aeroplane disintegrates, what was previously one becomes thousands of little pieces. It is no longer united. It no longer forms a whole. Instead, it is in smithereens.

Now let us reverse the process. The countless scattered fragments of the plane come together and form a single united whole. Every tiny piece is in its place and nothing is missing. But let us remember that this is only an illustration. We are not talking about an aeroplane but a human life, where all the parts of that life fit perfectly together and form a whole. This is integrity.

In a life of integrity no part of that life is out of step with any other part. There is no God/man tension, no body/soul tension, and no understanding/will tension. Let us take these three aspects one by one.

There is no God/man tension. The way the person lives is completely in line with what God wants. And we do not have to guess what God wants. It is memorably summarised for us in Micah 6:8 : 'He has shown you, O man, what is good; and what does the Lord require of you but to do justly, to love mercy, and to walk humbly with your God?' If, in a given situation, we feel about it what God does not *feel* about it, our emotion at that point is obviously illegitimate. However good I may feel in myself, if I am in any way unjust, or unkind and inconsiderate, or out of conscious communion with the Lord, my emotion is completely out of order.

There is no body/soul tension. If my body is doing one thing (for example, singing a great hymn with enthusiasm) but my soul is doing another (for example, feeling that I am doing a great job by singing like this), then my emotion at that moment is not at all pleasing to the Lord. Our Lord focuses on this inner contradiction in Matthew 7:21–29, where He makes some sobering predictions about the end of the world. At the last judgment there will be some people who will express their pleasure that they have spent their lives speaking in Christ's name, opposing evil, and doing wonderful things in His cause. In their brief lifetimes, this is what they have done with their bodies. But they will go to hell! And why is that? It is because their souls have been preoccupied with what *they* were doing, rather than with doing the Father's will out of obedience to Christ's teaching.

There is no understanding/will tension. There are two dangers here. The first is the danger of having an emotion (that is, a strong movement of the will, an inner 'Yes!' or 'No!') but of having no understanding of why that is so. The fact is that emotions can be manipulated. People can be made to have certain feelings without there being any reason for their feeling like that. It can be done by loud music with a strong beat or rhythm. It can be done by alcohol or other drugs. It can be done by the 'atmosphere' of a crowd. It can be done by the telling of a 'sob story' and a thousand other tricks. In each case the person feels something, and feels it deeply, but cannot tell you why they feel that way, even if they are given time to think about it. There is no integration between their understanding and their will. This is not how God intended men and women to be.

Another danger is the emotion that arises from a false understanding. We see an example of this in 1 Thessalonians 4:13–18. The believers at Thessalonica were grieving over their deceased members in a way which was little or no different from the way that unbelievers grieved over their bereavements. In addition, they were lacking the comfort and emotional support which the gospel offered. And why was this? It was because their understanding was faulty. They had not yet grasped the truth about what happens to believers at death. As a result their emotional life was not only unhelpful to themselves; it was displeasing to the Lord.

6. We now have some guidelines to help us have a practical approach to this subject

We have not said everything that there is to be said, but at least we are now in a position to understand the main thrust of what the Bible reveals about emotion, and how to make practical use of our new knowledge.

We know what emotions are—which is not true of most people around us, including very many of our fellow believers in Christ. It is also clear to us that we must do all that we can to encourage legitimate emotions and to reject illegitimate emotions. And this is something we can do, because we now know which are which.

We are also in a position to begin helping people with emotional problems, including ourselves. We will stress to them that however they feel, they must give themselves to obeying God's Word, so as to avoid the three tensions that we have mentioned above. We will also be realistic about the fact that many emotional problems have physical causes, as we have also seen above, and that these physical causes should be addressed. This may mean referring the person to the medical profession, or to someone experienced in helping those who are dependent on drugs. Most of all, we will focus on reshaping the person's thought life. This is because emotions are 'Yes!' or 'No!' responses to the thoughts that are going through our minds and, as we have also seen, ignorance or error provoke wrong and unhelpful emotions.

But teaching the people the truth is not enough. This is because, left to themselves, men and women are completely unable to desire it, to believe it, to love it, to treasure it and to live it out. Unconverted people need to be inwardly transformed; they need regenerating; they need a new nature; they need to be born again. Even converted people cannot continue or advance in godly understanding, feeling and living, unless the Holy Spirit works in their souls. But we have no control over the Holy Spirit. All we can do is to pray for His working. Like the apostles of old, therefore, we must 'give ourselves continually to prayer and to the ministry of the word' (Acts 6:4)—in that order!

But how can we help others if we are not emotionally stable ourselves? Full inward and outward obedience to God's Word must be our moment-by-moment priority. In addition, because body and soul are inter-dependent, and interact and co-act, we must take every concrete step we can to ensure that we are as physically healthy as possible. We must also feed our minds, filling them with whatever is true, noble, just, pure, lovely, of good report, virtuous and praiseworthy. If we do this, and also focus on learning from every godly example we see, we are assured that the God of peace will be with us (see Philippians 4:8–9). Godly emotion will be our daily experience.

2. The Holy Spirit's Work in the Soul

Emotions, then, are strong movements of the will. But why do people's emotions differ so much? For example, I know countless people who go into ecstasy when their favourite football team scores a goal, while I find myself rather bored by the whole thing. Other people stand deeply moved in front of a painting and are grieved that so many of their friends can see nothing in it. Yet others find unspeakable pleasure in walking in the countryside, in sharp contrast to those who flee all contact with nature for the bright lights and thrills of the city

A doctor I know was excited to learn that he could have classical music piped to the waiting room in his surgery. It would, he thought, calm everyone down, especially if they were nervous. The outcome was very different from what he expected. His practice was inundated with complaints. Almost no one wanted to hear classical music while they were waited to see the doctor. Easy listening, yes! Pop music, yes! But classical music? No! No! Absolutely not!

The Bible is very clear that we are all very different from one another. We have different characters, different temperaments, different interests and different gifts. It is not strange, then, that we should have widely differing emotions. What provokes a strong inner 'Yes!' in one person may easily stir up an equally strong 'No!' in another. There is no mystery here.

But we cannot answer the question so easily when it comes to the things of God. Countless people are never 'lost in wonder, love and praise'[8] before the living God. They have no desire to know Him, and find no pleasure in reading His Word or hearing it preached. His Son, Jesus Christ, is not precious to them. Their sin does not particularly trouble them. They do not have praying hearts. Death approaches, but they seldom ask what lies beyond it. They pass their short time on earth seeking significance, loving their family and friends, being as comfortable and as happy as they can, and only very occasionally asking any ultimate questions at all.

There are others, however, who are completely different. God is constantly in their thoughts. They love Him, worship Him, want to please Him, and cannot keep their distance from Him. Their rebellion against Him has been quelled and they desire from the heart to serve His Son, Jesus Christ. They treasure Christ's cross and rejoice in the forgiveness of sins that they have received through Him. They feel that they can never have enough of the Bible. They love to pray. They look forward to an eternity where all is holy and happy, and where they can at last offer to the Lord the praise that He deserves.

Why is there is such a radical difference between these two sets of people? Is it just one more example of differing temperaments and inclinations? This cannot be the answer because nobody, left to themself, has any desire for God. The Bible is dogmatic on this point. All men and women know that God exists. They know that He is their invisible, eternal and powerful Creator, and that at the end of time He will be their Judge. But they would rather serve themselves than serve Him, whatever may be the consequences. They are spiritually dead, and cannot stir their lifeless souls to want Him more than anything else in the whole universe.

The new birth

People who trust Christ alone for their salvation and who have God as their Heavenly Father have not become like this simply because they are naturally more 'religious' than others. It is because God Himself has intervened in their life. They have been regenerated. In the words of Jesus Himself, the Holy Spirit has done something to them and they have been 'born again' (John 3:1–21).

Regeneration is an act of God by which He gives spiritual life to a person, making them into 'a new creation' (2 Corinthians 5:17). As a result they are permanently changed within their soul, and the whole of their life goes in a new direction. As we have seen, the soul is composed of two parts, the understanding and the will. The regenerated person therefore sees things differently and chooses differently. The first sign of their regeneration is that they receive Christ, believe on Him, and become children of God (John 1:12–13).

Back in the fourth century Augustine of Hippo[9] likened regeneration to the movement of a weathercock. If the wind blows from the East, it faces East. If it blows from the West, it faces West. The cock does not move itself, but is moved by the wind. The human will is moved in the same way. If unconverted winds blow through a soul, that person will face in an unconverted direction and will make the choices that unconverted people make. If however a converted wind blows through the soul, that person will face in a converted direction and will make the choices that converted people make. Everything depends on which wind is blowing through the soul.

But how, precisely, does the Holy Spirit blow through the soul? Does He work directly, or does He use means? It is important for us to answer this question. If we don't, how will we ever get close to understanding regeneration? But there is something else: regeneration is the first spiritual experience that a child of God has, so it is safe to assume that subsequent spiritual experiences will probably follow a similar pattern. By knowing more about regeneration in particular we may know more about spiritual experiences in general.

Although it was more nuanced and complex than I can present here, the overall belief and teaching of the great Reformer, Martin Luther,[10] was that the Holy Spirit does not work directly on the human soul, but that He uses an instrument to bring about the new birth. That instrument, or means, is the Bible. Luther was well aware that he, as a mere man, could never change anyone inwardly. But if he preached the Word of God, the work would get done. The miracle would take place. Men and women, boys and girls, would be transformed for ever, just as long as they were put in the presence of the preached Word.

We owe more to Luther than any of us can ever calculate, and I do not for a moment intend to tarnish his memory. But I cannot hide the fact that on this point the general tenor of his teaching was wrong. It is true that a mere man cannot bring about the new birth. But, on its own, nor can the Bible. The Bible is certainly the Word of God, and when it is preached, the mind of God is proclaimed in people's hearing. Undoubtedly more is happening at that moment than human minds can ever realise, but that does not mean that a saving work of God is automatically going on in the hearts of the hearers. For that to happen, something else is required. When the gospel has success, we can't write about it as Luther did.

Luther had fallen into the error that is called 'mediate regeneration'.[11] This may not interest you very much, and you may believe that this chapter is of no relevance to you. I invite you to think again. Mediate regeneration eventually did terrible damage to the Lutheran movement. The trouble is that this error is on the march once more and is not meeting with much resistance. It has already taken over vast sectors of British Evangelicalism. It has captured countless preachers, churches, training courses and Bible-teaching organisations. If we don't wake up, it will soon take us over completely. From then on, gospel work in this country will be ruined. This will be because of its failure to understand the nature of genuine spiritual experience.

The error

Mediate regeneration teaches that when the Holy Spirit transforms somebody into a new creature in Christ, He uses an instrument to bring this about. That instrument is the Word—the Holy Scriptures. The work of the Spirit is so intimately connected to His instrument, that we can say that the Word of God actually contains the converting power of the Holy Spirit. If you let the Word loose, you are letting the Holy Spirit loose.

To put it another way: the Spirit, or the principle of new life, is shut up in the Word, just as the life-giving germ is shut up in the dry seed. Just sow the seed and people will get converted! If they don't, it will be because they have persistently turned away the appeals of God's Spirit coming to them through that Word. His power is resident in the Word, but that power has been resisted. Where the gospel has little success, there is a human explanation.

The truth

This, however, is not what the Bible teaches. The truth is that the Holy Spirit does not work *through* the Word ('per verbum', as our forefathers would say). In fact, if He wishes, He can even work without the Word.[12] He can! He is, after all, sovereign, and so can use the Word—or *not* use the Word—as He pleases. Normally, however, His operation *accompanies* the Word ('cum verbo'). The Word and the Spirit work together.

Regeneration is a supernatural enlightenment of the human soul brought about by the direct and immediate energy of the Holy Spirit working within that soul. There is nothing 'mediate' about it. It is not brought about by some influence or instruction from outside, but by the implanting of new spiritual life inside. The Holy Spirit does not work by the Word *upon* the will, but *in* the will itself, changing a person's desires and giving to the active powers of his soul a completely new direction. In simple English, God touches a person in their heart of hearts and changes them for ever. He Himself does something in their innermost being, without using an instrument. It is a one-to-one between God and the person involved. There is no go-between.

Does this mean that God simply 'zaps' people and they become Christians? No; we can put what happens like this. A person hears the gospel proclaimed to them from the Bible. While this is happening, God works directly in their soul. They are changed inside. The Holy Spirit gives them sight, but what they see is the truth of the Word. The Holy Spirit gives them hearing, but what they hear is the voice of Christ in the Word. The Holy Spirit gives them feeling, but what they come to love is the Word. The Holy Spirit gives them a new nature, and, as a result, they now freely choose to embrace Jesus Christ, who is presented to them in the Word.

Previously, they may well have understood a great deal of what the Word was saying, but the power and overwhelming eternal importance of it never struck them. Now their understanding is enlightened. Previously they had no love for the things of God; now they see the beauty of them and love them in the depths of their soul. Previously they chose to live without God; now they choose Him as the Lord of their life, and desire to live in glad obedience to Him. A miracle has taken place! It has happened because of a direct and life-giving act of God the Holy Spirit. Without this act, they would have remained as they were. The fact that some believe, while others remain in unbelief, thus has a divine explanation.

The Bible

Lutheranism got it wrong. What has just been outlined is clearly the Bible's teaching. Throughout its pages the influence of the Spirit is distinguished from that of the Word (John 6:45, 64–65; 1 Corinthians 2:12–15; 1 Thessalonians 1:5–6). No one can receive the truth unless God works in them (Psalm 119:18; Ephesians 1:17). This work is internal (Philippians 2:13; Hebrews 13:21). We must never think that the gift of the Spirit and the gift of the Word are the same thing, or that the Spirit and the Word work in the same way (John 14:16; 1 Corinthians 3:16, 6:19, Ephesians 1:19, 3:7, 4:30). The Bible's teaching on this subject is encapsulated in Acts 16:14. In Greek this reads like this: 'And a certain woman named Lydia … was hearing us, whose heart the Lord opened up completely, with the result that she heeded to the things being spoken by Paul.' Her opened heart is not attributed to the Word she was listening to, but to an act of the Lord Himself! It was from that moment that she gave the Word her full attention and took on board its message.

Elsewhere the apostle Paul writes about regeneration in the following way: 'It is the God who commanded light to shine out of darkness who has shone in our hearts to give the light of the knowledge of the glory of God in the face of Jesus

Christ' (2 Corinthians 4:6). God did it! But Paul is clearly speaking of something that accompanied the preaching of the Word, because this verse is found in the middle of a section dealing with that very subject!

But aren't there verses that teach equally clearly that it is the Word that brings about regeneration? Yes, some verses do give that impression. But if we look at them more closely, we shall see them in a different light. For example, James 1:18 says that 'of his own will he brought us forth by the word of truth'. This is a reference, however, not to the act of germination (where a new life comes into being) but to the moment of birth (where the new life becomes visible).[13] 1 Peter 1:23 is almost certainly to be understood in the same way. It says that we have 'been born again, not of corruptible seed but incorruptible, through the word of God which lives and abides for ever.' Conception and birth are not the same thing!

Two mind-sets

'So what?' you may say, 'Isn't all this just a mere arguing about words and irrelevant concepts?' If that was the case, I would never have written this chapter. The fact is that your beliefs about this subject will affect your personal life, your church life and your evangelism.

Sooner or later, those who believe in mediate regeneration develop a certain mind-set. We can already see this in the Evangelicalism which is all around us. It goes like this: 'As long as we sow the Word, concentrating on making its meaning clear, spiritual work will get done. God's call will provoke a response in those who listen to us, except among those who persistently resist that call. It's enough to get the Word out. As long as we do that well, what more can we do?' The great emphasis among those of this mind-set is therefore on what they call 'Word ministry.'

A biblical mind-set ticks completely differently. It goes like this:

- Although the Word can bring a new spiritual life to birth and visibility, it can never bring about the generation of that new life. *God Himself* must do that, by a direct action of His Spirit within the human soul.

- We can preach, teach, persuade and print until we are blue in the face, but no spiritual work will get done in human hearts unless *the Lord Himself* accompanies the Word. This He is normally pleased to do; but we have no mandate to take the ordinary operations of the Spirit for granted. The fact remains that all men and women are spiritually dead, and will remain so for ever, unless the Lord personally brings them to life.

- It is not enough then to sow the Word, making its meaning plain while we do so. We must have dealings with God, pleading with Him to do what only He can do, that is, to work by direct action within people's souls

Where the biblical mind-set rules

Where the biblical mind-set rules, you will find preachers who 'pray through'—men who strive and agonise and prevail in prayer, so as to be sure that the Lord will accompany their preaching in an obvious way.

Where the biblical mind-set rules, you will find crowded prayer meetings filled with believers who long for unconverted people to be saved and for converted people to be encouraged and strengthened. This being so, they set out together to storm the throne of grace, determined that by sheer importunity they will persuade their gracious and willing God to accompany the Word to be preached.

Where the biblical mind-set rules, you will find gatherings of Christians beseeching their Lord to pour out His Spirit in awakening power. Of course you will! They understand all too well that no spiritual work will get done anywhere, however much sowing takes place, unless the Lord Himself changes rebellious hearts and gives to them spiritual life and appetite.

Where the biblical mind-set rules, you will find an appreciation of felt religion, even during those periods where there is no sign of any widespread revival on the horizon. When the Holy Spirit is not doing an extraordinary work (that is, His ordinary work with increased intensity), His ordinary work continues, and it is His ordinary work to enlighten the mind, to stir up holy emotions and to give spiritual experiences. Although He normally does this by accompanying the Word, He can well do it without the Word, which explains a whole host of events in the illustrious history of the Christian church.

But the biblical mind-set does not rule. Most British preachers study more than they pray. Countless believers do not go regularly to church prayer-meetings, or, if they do, they fail to plead with God for His blessing upon the preaching. Prayer for revival has almost left us. There is little understanding that strong, personal dealings with God are part and parcel of normal, daily Christian experience. The error of mediate regeneration is slowly but surely strangling us, and things will go from bad to worse unless we repent.

Something else

But there is something else. Once we are clear about immediate regeneration we begin to understand the experiences of our fellow believers whose spiritual life has begin in an unusual way. To close this chapter, and to illustrate what I am trying to say, I would like to give you three examples.

A middle-aged couple I know were lying in bed and talking about their lives. Neither of them had ever had much contact with the gospel, nor did they have any spiritual interest. But the wife was unwell and was wondering why such awful things were happening to her. 'I don't know,' she said, 'I can't make sense of it all.'

'But I can,' said her husband. 'There has got to be Someone out there who is greater than we are, and who is working things in such a way that we poor people will recognise his worth.'

What the husband said was as much a surprise to him as it was to his wife! The thought had flashed into his mind with a clarity that convinced him of its truth. From that moment on he and his wife became spiritually serious, and it was not long afterwards that they came into contact with Bible-believing friends and were converted. How can you explain what happened to him and his wife if you do not believe in immediate regeneration?

A friend of mine who is an acknowledged intellectual told me that after spending his childhood in a Christian family he became an outspoken atheist, totally opposed to what his parents wanted him to believe. Inwardly, however, he had occasional moments where his conscience convinced him that God existed, although his considerable intellect strongly contradicted the idea. One such moment threw him into complete turmoil. It happened on a station where, having waved goodbye to his girlfriend, he turned to return home. There on the platform he made up his mind to reopen the whole question of the existence of God.

He felt conscious that God existed and yet could not be convinced intellectually. In genuine distress at the enigma of his position he found himself saying, 'O God, I do not at this moment actually believe in you. But if you *are* there, *you* will have to find me, because, on my own, I am completely unable to find you.'

It was very shortly afterwards that he turned to the Scriptures, read the laws that were given to ancient Israel, and was so struck by their wisdom, balance and justice, that he became convinced of their divine origin. Not long after that he came, through Jesus Christ, to know personally the living and true God revealed in the Bible. His sharp mind and literary gifts are now used in expounding the Christian faith and applying its teaching to the modern world. But how can you explain what happened to him if you do not believe that the Holy Spirit works immediately on the soul from within, bringing people to say 'Yes!' to what they previously rejected with a steadfast 'No!'?

A final example concerns a young lady who was waiting for me before a Sunday morning service. I had never met her before, but she told me that something had happened to her, that she didn't know what it was, and that she felt that she ought to tell me about it.

'I have just got engaged,' she said, 'but on the day of my engagement my fiancé told me that he was a spiritist medium. This made me very scared and I didn't know what to do. So I prayed to God to rescue me—and He has come into me. He has! He has! And I can feel that He has!'

Not knowing what to say, I told the young lady that it would be a good idea if she stayed for the service and that we spent some time talking afterwards. This she consented to do. 'That's it!' she said, as we talked about the sermon in which I had preached Christ and His cross, 'That's it! It's true, it's all true!' She openly professed Christ, broke off her engagement, and was soon baptised and received into membership of the church.

Speaking for myself, I believe that God *did* come into this young lady in the way that she said, which I certainly could not believe if I held to the error of mediate regeneration.

Regeneration is the first of our spiritual experiences, and teaches us that the Holy Spirit's work in the human soul is immediate and direct. This is something we must remember when we consider every subsequent spiritual experience. If we do not, all our thinking about how God deals with us will go seriously astray.

A postscript

The first draft of this chapter finished with the sentence above. I then sent the chapter to a good friend of mine and asked him to comment on its readability. This he duly did, but his e-mail also contained some personal information which, I believe, might be of interest to some readers. So here are some extracts from that e-mail, published here with my friend's permission:

'I was blown away by this chapter because you spoke right into my own experience! You have probably heard the testimony of my conversion a couple of times, but there is a part I have kept hidden from most people. Why keep it hidden? There are a couple of reasons. The main reason lies in harmony with your book, in that the reaction I received from folk I shared this with was, in the main, negative rather than positive, i.e. it was implied that it cannot have been a work of God since the Spirit only works through the Word. And at that point I was certainly not reading the Scriptures or hearing the gospel. This negative answer has never really sat well with me ...

'On a very windy night in the winter of 2006/7 I was lying in bed and felt compelled to go for a walk. I initially resisted; it was cold, windy and it was the middle of the night. When I left my front door I didn't know or care if God existed. By the time I returned I not only knew He existed, but I had met with Him and I had a new hunger to know more of Him. I spoke to the God whom I had ignored all my life to ask Him to help me with a battle I had been in for some time and was losing. I never heard an audible voice, neither did I see anything with my eyes; logically I couldn't explain why, but I knew I had met with God. How could I know that with such conviction? How did I know to go to Him for help? How did I know that God was going to give me strength to win this battle? (He did!). How could all this just happen out of the blue? Within a short time, by the Lord's leading, I was reading Mark's Gospel and learning about Jesus at the local Evangelical Church.

'Don't be concerned that I am pinning my salvation on this experience. I'm not; it is in the finished work of Christ alone that my hope is found. But I am convinced that the Holy Spirit broke into my life initially without the use of His Word, and looking back I can see evidence that He had been at work long before this.'

How do you react when you read something like this? All I can say is that I thank God for the Holy Spirit's immediate and direct work within the soul, both initially and throughout the Christian life.

3. Assurance of salvation

Such as truly believe in the Lord Jesus … may in this life be certainly assured that they are in the state of grace, and may rejoice in the hope of the glory of God; which hope shall never make them ashamed.

THE WESTMINSTER CONFESSION OF FAITH[14]

We have been considering the Holy Spirit's work in the soul and have had a lot to say about regeneration, otherwise known as the new birth. This is the first of our spiritual experiences. But it is not the last. Once someone has become a true Christian they may know with certainty that they are a child of God, that all their sins have been pardoned, that they have passed from spiritual death to eternal life, and that they are bound for heaven. In short, they may know that the Son of God loves them and has given Himself for them. They may go through life with *assurance*. This spiritual experience, together with the joy and relief that accompany it, is the birthright of every believer.[15]

Some believers lack assurance

Yet it is a fact that some regenerate people lack this assurance. All their hopes of being accepted by God depend on Jesus Christ. But they do not feel saved. They have no sense of being at peace with God. They go through life filled with self-questioning and doubts. Their constant question is, 'Am I a true Christian, or am I a counterfeit? Am I truly one of those who are accepted by God, or am I deceiving myself?'

Why should this be so?

We saw in chapter 1 that if a person is ignorant or ill-informed, their emotions will become skewed. Emotions are, after all, responses to the thoughts which are going through our heads. They are strong movements of the will by which we say 'Yes!' or 'No!' to those thoughts. If the thoughts are inaccurate, the emotions will not be valid. If something is to be *felt* as it should, it must be *known* as it should.

1) Now some Christians, because of their upbringing, or the teaching they have received, look upon the very idea of assurance with suspicion. To them, any claim to be sure of one's salvation is presumptuous. They think that only a shallow person would make a claim like that. Surely no one who knows anything about the deceitfulness of the human heart could be so cocksure. How often we have been 'sure' of things which later proved not to be certain at all!

Such people are not wrong about how easily misled the human heart can be. But they are completely wrong about assurance. The Bible makes it plain that such assurance is the believer's normal experience. The believers who are found on the pages of Scripture were not filled with self-questioning. They had plenty of emotional trouble. They were not strangers to sorrow. They frequently had cause to mourn over the sin which remained in their lives. They experienced opposition and adversity, and frequent heartbreak over the state of the church. But they did not doubt their own acceptance with God. They were confident of it, as is plain from such passages as Romans 5:1–2, Galatians 2:20, 2 Timothy 4:7–8 and 1 John 3:14. Lack of assurance is not something that God's Word expects a true believer to experience.

2) Some Christians do not enjoy assurance because they are put off by their failures and sins. They see their ungodliness, think about it, and lose their peace. 'If I was a true Christian,' they say, 'these things would simply not be found in my life. Can I really be a person indwelt by the Holy Spirit when I see so many examples of unholiness in my thoughts, words and actions?'

Once more, these people are an example of faulty thinking leading to illegitimate feeling. If they had a better understanding of what Christ has done by His life, death and resurrection, they would not argue in this way. I must not think that I am more acceptable to God on the days that I live well, but less acceptable to Him on the days that I fail and live badly. My own performance has never been the ground upon which God accepts me. Nor will it ever be.

The life which I should have lived, but have not, *Christ* lived for me. That remains true however I may have lived today. The penalty for my sins was *completely* carried by Christ, so there is no penalty of any sort for me to carry, today or any other day. This remains true whether today was a 'success' or not. My daily performance has no effect on my acceptance with God. That rests entirely on what Christ has done on my behalf. His work is over, has been accepted, and will never be repeated. The benefit of what He has done was reckoned to my account the moment I believed. As long as I depend on Him, I have nothing to fear—even when my faith is weak, defective and shaken. It is not to strong believers, but to *believers* plain and simple that the benefits of His redemption flow.

3) There is a third reason why some believers do not have assurance. Once more, it is to do with what goes through their minds. They have a stereotyped view of conversion. They hear others tell how they came to Christ and, because their own experience does not fit into what appears to be the normal pattern, they doubt whether their conversion has been real.

Such Christians need to have their thoughts corrected. They need to recognise that no two testimonies are the same. Some people are awakened from their spiritual death by a trumpet call—a dramatic and traumatic experience. Others are woken up gradually. Yet others are awakened as a mother wakens her sleeping infant—with a kiss. In other words, their experience is gentle and its stages are not easily defined. The *manner* of awakening is not important. The real issue is whether a person has been awakened at all.

In all true conversions there are two elements. There is some consciousness of sin and of the need to be reconciled to God. There is also some grasp of the sufficiency of Christ to be the sinner's Saviour, by virtue of His life, death and resurrection. These two elements move the sinner to cast themself on Christ, and to find in Him all their hopes of being accepted by God.

This does not mean that all believers have experienced conviction of sin to the same degree. Some have not had the soul-shaking experiences that others have gone through. But this should not make them doubt the genuineness of their conversion. Were they sufficiently convinced of their sin to seek the mercy of God in Christ? That is the single point of importance. Your own individual road to Christ does not matter, but the destination is vital. Whatever route you have come by, do you have faith in the Lord Jesus Christ *now*?

If you have come from a Christian family it is particularly important that you should look at things in this way. You have been taught the truth of the gospel from your earliest years. It is quite possible that you cannot recall precisely when you came to trust Christ in a personal way. It may well have happened before your character was fully formed. Perhaps you cannot even remember a time when you did *not* love and trust Him. Do not let this trouble you, and do not be haunted by the more definable experiences of others. If, as you read this, you are depending for your acceptance with God entirely upon the person and work of the Lord Jesus Christ, you are a Christian indeed. You do not need to let uncertainty spoil your joy for a moment longer.

4) A fourth reason for lack of assurance is that some Christians mix up 'faith' and 'strong faith'. They see that their

lives are not as saintly as the lives of others, and therefore wonder whether they are truly children of God. How close to God the other person appears to be! How strong in faith and advanced in knowledge! How mighty they are in prayer! What zeal they have! What graces are seen in their life! When we see such outstanding men and women of God we are very tempted to say, 'I am not in the same class at all. My own spiritual life is so poor in comparison. My life and theirs are a thousand miles apart. Perhaps I do not have *any* spiritual life'.

This is quite the wrong conclusion to reach. Certainly I am a poor specimen, but that does not mean that I am not a Christian at all. My weakness should grieve me. It should break my heart. But it should not take away my assurance. It is true that I am not what I should be. But it is equally true that I am not what I used to be! I am a believer, albeit an immature one. I am nothing in Christian stature when compared to others. But I draw all my hope from the fact that God justifies the ungodly.[16] For my acceptance with God I do not rely on the high quality of my Christian life, but on the finished work of Christ on my behalf.

It is this reliance which distinguishes true believers from unbelievers. No Christian can ever be perfect in this life. There will always be room for improvement. Every day sees every Christian repenting over their remaining deficiencies. They will never be what they most deeply want to be. But their faith is in Christ and, for Christ's sake, God accepts them. It is that fact alone which makes their Christian life valid. It means that however poor they may be when compared with others, they need never doubt the certainty of their acceptance with God.

Some people have false assurance

We have seen that some people who are entitled to a feeling of assurance do not have it. The opposite is also true. There are some people who are *not* entitled to it who *do* have it. They are sure that they are true Christians, although they are not. They are self-deceived. They have false assurance.

How does this awful situation arise? Their feelings mislead them because their thoughts are in error. They are mistaken about what is the proof of being a true believer. As evidence of their salvation they accept certain traits which the Bible flatly rejects. Because they misunderstand what are the signs of being a true Christian, they come to misguided conclusions about their own standing with God.

1) Let us give some examples. In the last few decades there has grown the widespread conviction that God is restoring to the churches certain miraculous gifts which have been absent since the days of the apostles. Such gifts are held to include the power to speak in tongues which have never been learned, and the power to expel demons from those whose personalities are controlled by them. Among those who lay claim to these gifts are some who argue that they could never possess them if they were not true believers. Does not their very enjoyment of gifts given by the Holy Spirit prove that He is at work in their lives?

It is beyond the purpose of this book to examine whether these gifts are real or not. Let us assume for the moment that they are. It still does not follow that those who possess them are true Christians. Judas had all the miraculous gifts enjoyed by the other apostles. But it turned out in the end that his spiritual experience was not genuine, and so he was finally lost. Jesus Himself predicted that many of those who will be eternally in hell will be those who, during their lifetime, exercised spiritual gifts in His name (Matthew 7:22). The possession of spiritual gifts tells us nothing about the person who has them. They are not proof of super spirituality because they are not even proof of the most basic spiritual change of all.

2) We can give many other examples of a similar sort of reasoning. There are those who conclude that they are true Christians simply because they believe all that the Bible teaches. But we need to remember that it is possible to know the Bible from end to end, and even to believe it, and not to know the power of its message in your life. By studying the Bible it is even possible to become an expert in all aspects of Christian experience, and to describe almost every situation and emotion which a genuine believer may go through—and yet not be a genuine believer yourself!

After all, although the Bible is not like any other book, it can be studied like any other book. Its contents can be mastered, charted, systematised, remembered and recited without the reader ever coming to personal repentance towards God and faith in our Lord Jesus Christ. Countless numbers of us knew exactly what God required of us long before we became Christians. We were not strangers to the truth, but our faith was not yet relying on a *Person*!

3) Some people, while reading or hearing the Bible, have come under conviction of sin. They have been shaken by

the realisation that they are estranged from God and under His wrath. Sometimes this conviction of sin has been of extraordinary intensity and has lasted weeks and months. The experience has been almost infinitely traumatic.

Many who have had such an experience have assumed that they have been converted. But we must realise that conviction of sin and conversion are not the same thing. There is more to conversion than seeing myself as a sinner. The realisation must drive me to cast myself on Christ. If it does not, I cannot call myself a Christian, because I have neither repented nor believed.

On the other hand, if the conviction is not at all intense, but is none the less sufficient to move me to lay hold on the Saviour, it is enough. In fact it is quite common for believers to have had a less intense conviction of sin than those who have never come to Christ. A few minutes' reflection will reveal why this is so. Their sense of sin makes them seek pardon. When they find it, their hearts are flooded with peace. But for the others there is no relief for their sense of guilt. Because they never seek pardon, it may go to an intensity never experienced by a true Christian. It may, as in the case of Judas, even drive them to suicide. They thus die in despair and are ushered into eternity knowing nothing of what it means to be forgiven.

4) It is the same with disillusionment with the world. There are millions of disappointed people on this planet. They have found no lasting happiness here. They are aware that all earth's joys are fleeting. All that it promises comes

to nothing. They feel that life is empty and see themselves as alone. Very often they are filled with unabated pessimism and bitterness.

On the face of it, it may look as if such people are Christians, or are very close to being so. Nothing could be further from the truth. There is more to being a Christian than discovering that this life is empty. The great feature of believers is that they consider everything as worthless when compared with *Christ*. They will turn their back on everything else for the greater price of knowing *Him* (Philippians 3:1–11). It is because of the greater and eternal joys to be found in Christ that they have such a low view of what the world offers. The new affection drives out the old. Their lives are thus the exact opposite of those who are disillusioned with the world. They are not lives of unrelieved pessimism. The eyes of every believer are on the heavenly destination and the eternal home. It is in *that* light that this world is seen to be transient, and unable to offer either solid joys or lasting treasure.

True assurance

False assurance is the result of mistaking what are the characteristics of a true Christian. How then does *true* assurance come? How may I discover whether I am a true believer or whether I am deceiving myself?

The way to be sure is to examine both the New Testament and myself at the same time. The New Testament gives a clear picture of what a true Christian is like. With that in mind, I look at myself. Do I find that the New Testament picture and what I see in my own life are one and the same?

In other words, when I read the New Testament's description of a Christian, do I find that it is describing *me*? If so, there can be no doubt that I am a true child of God, and that any fears I have about my standing with God are groundless. But if the two pictures do not tally, it is evident that I am not a believer. It is time for me to repent of my sins and to cast myself on the mercy of God which is freely offered to me in His Son.

1) What *is* the picture which the New Testament gives of a true believer? First of all, a Christian is someone who has faith in the Lord Jesus Christ (Acts 20:21). They have heard about Christ and are convinced that they have heard the truth. They move from this to actually put their trust in Christ. They approach Him and rely upon Him *as a person* to secure their acceptance with God.

The easiest way to discover whether I have such faith is to examine my prayers. I am God's creature, with a polluted nature and many actual sins of thought, word and deed. The eternal God is my Creator and 'of purer eyes than to behold evil' (Habakkuk 1:13). Yet I pray to Him, approach Him, and expect to be heard and received. On what basis? Why should He pay attention to *me*?

If I expect Him to hear and receive me on the basis of the length or sincerity of my prayer, or on the basis of my good life, or my religion, or my intentions, or my church affiliation, or my need, or my weakness, or anything like that *whatever*—then I must face the fact that these are the things on which I rely for my acceptance with God. My trust is in them, and I do not fit the picture of a New Testament believer.

When true believers call upon God they are painfully conscious of the awfulness of their sin, and they remember with relief that God's Son has died for sinners and has carried their just penalty. All their hopes of being heard depend on the fact that God justifies the ungodly, and that He reckons the righteousness of Christ to the account of all who come to Him as Saviour. True believers approach God as sinners. They are all too well aware that they should be excluded from heaven, but plead the fact that there is One there who speaks on behalf of sinners and guarantees their acceptance. If these considerations, and these considerations *alone*, are the basis of my expectancy of having access to God's throne, it is clear that my faith is in Christ. I have the first mark of a child of God.

2) The second distinguishing mark of a true Christian, according to the New Testament, is that they have a certain attitude to indwelling sin. What is my attitude to the plain fact that, even now, I do not keep the moral law of God? I have fallen short of His demands. I have even broken through His law by doing those things which He forbids. This is true of my outward actions, but also of my inmost thoughts and motives. Do I greet this information with apathy? Is it only of slight interest to me? Do I yawn and say that 'I have heard it all before'?

Or does the reminder trouble me? Does it sometimes break my heart and cause me to cry out with inward despair? Am I ever bewildered by the fact that the things I do not want to do are the very things that I do, and the things I want so much to do are too often the very duties in which I fail? Am I ever filled with dismay at the contradiction between what I *want* to be, and what in practice I *am*? Do I long—deeply and often—to be different?

It is in precisely such terms, and with deep feeling, that Paul describes his own experience as a Christian in Romans 7:14–25. This is how the heart of a child of God operates. Apathy in the face of sin is the badge of the lost. Agony caused by indwelling sin is a marked feature of a true Christian. Is it a feature of me?

3) A third mark of a Christian is brotherly love: 'We know that we have passed from death to life, because we love the brethren' (1 John 3:14). How do we behave towards those whom we love best? We consider their wishes, seek their welfare and are jealous for their reputations. We are willing to make almost any sacrifice to help them. We cannot keep them out of our thoughts for very long, and can hardly wait to be in their company again.

This is the way that true believers behave towards each other. They submit to one another and seek each other's good. This love is not qualified or altered when the other person is unlovely, or is temperamentally difficult. The bonds which unite Christians are bonds of mutual understanding and forgiveness. This remains the case however often the other has disappointed or offended me, or frustrated my plans and ambitions. My fellow believer is my *brother* or *sister*. I will not be quick to judge them harshly, whatever provocations they may bring my way. We are members of the same family, bought with the same blood, indwelt by the same Spirit, and bound for the same heavenly destination. We belong to one another, for time and for eternity.

It is true that I am obliged to love my neighbour as myself. Christians are not the only people I must love. Yet my love for fellow-believers is different. My attitudes and behaviour towards them reveal my sense of oneness with them. If they do not, it is because I am *not* one of them. I do not have the third distinctive mark of a genuine believer. Anyone who is not burning with love for those whose faith is in Christ alone is misleading themselves, if they consider themselves to be one of their number.

The work of the Spirit

It is by looking at these marks of a Christian which the New Testament provides that we are able to obey the command, 'Examine yourselves, as to whether you are in the faith' (2 Corinthians 13:5). Assurance comes by self-examination, and it is by the same process that false assurance is destroyed.

Yet there are passages in the New Testament which teach that our assurance is given to us by the Holy Spirit. For instance, Paul writes, 'The Spirit himself bears witness with our spirit that we are children of God' (Romans 8:16; see Galatians 4:6). What does that mean? And how does it fit in with our assertion that self-examination is the way to assurance?

To answer this we must remember that the Holy Spirit is the Author of the Scriptures. It is He who moved the human authors to pen what they wrote. This means that it is *He* who, ultimately, has provided the description of true believers that we have been considering.

Having Himself given us these definite marks of a true Christian, it would be exceedingly strange if the Holy Spirit made no use of them in bringing us to assurance. The way that He works is this. We read in the Scriptures what a true believer looks like. After a little while we are driven to the conclusion that we are reading about *ourselves*. With some feeling we say to ourselves, 'That description of a true Christian is a description of *me*!' The thought is borne in upon us with conviction. It is carried home to our hearts and we become confident that a general description on the pages of the Bible is an accurate description of our own personal lives. We are entirely persuaded that we are the children of God being spoken about. Something written in cold print becomes to us both heart-warming and reassuring. It becomes a source of daily strength and comfort.

What is the explanation of all this? It is the work of the Holy Spirit. The divine Author takes hold of the very Word that He has inspired and uses it to bring assurance into the lives of those He has changed. He does not persuade us of our standing of God in a vacuum, but applies to us the evidences which He Himself has caused to be written in His Word. *This* is the way that the Holy Spirit convinces us that we are the children of God.

Assurance, then, does not come about by the Word alone. It is not a simple deduction from an open Bible. Nor does it come about by the Holy Spirit alone. It comes about as the Holy Spirit *accompanies* the Word. It was by exactly this means that we were first brought to faith in Christ in, as we saw in chapter 2. All our spiritual convictions were born in us by similar operations. This is how the work of God proceeds in the human heart. His work of assurance is no departure from His normal way of working. The experience is wonderful. It fills us with enduring joy. But it is not a special experience reserved for a small elite. It does not fall into the category of 'an extraordinary operation of the Spirit'. Assurance is the birthright of every child of God.

All these things being so, we would expect that the more a Christian is exposed to the Word which the Spirit uses, the more sure they will be of their standing with God. The opposite is also true: we may expect assurance to decrease if the believer should ever neglect God's Word, or turn away from it. The experiences of Christians throughout the last two thousand years confirm this conclusion completely.

A final question

This does, however, raise a final question. What about those believers who, for one reason or another, no longer have access to the Word? Being deprived of the Word, are they also deprived of assurance?

This is a question of huge importance, especially for our brothers and sisters in Christ who are being persecuted. Countless numbers of them are in prison, and for some of these there will never be any release. The years will go by and they will die without ever seeing a Bible again. We have said above that the way to be sure of one's salvation is 'to examine both the New Testament and myself at the same time', but these dear believers do not have the New Testament! We have also stressed that real certainty springs up in our hearts as the Holy Spirit accompanies the Word. Does all this mean that those who most need such inward comfort can never have it?

We can thank our Heavenly Father that persecuted believers do not lack assurance—it is precisely because they *are* sure of their salvation that they endure what they have to bear. How else would they remain faithful to Christ year after year, enduring shame, privation, torture, and often execution? In this twenty-first century someone dies for Christ every eleven minutes. The heart's cry of every one of them is one of personal certainty and assurance:

'I ... suffer these things; nevertheless I am not ashamed, for I know whom I have believed and am persuaded that he is able to keep what I have committed to him until that day' (2 Timothy 1:12).

'I have fought the good fight, I have finished the race, I have kept the faith. Finally, there is laid up for me the crown of righteousness, which the Lord, the righteous Judge, will give to me on that day, and not only to me but also to all who have loved his appearing' (2 Timothy 4:7–8).

Our brothers and sisters who suffer persecution are not super-Christians. They are ordinary believers who have heard the gospel, accepted it as true, and have entrusted themselves to Christ as Lord and Saviour, believing that His promise to save them is trustworthy. Like us, their first assurance was a wavering and unsteady experience, simply because their faith in the bare word of God was hesitant and fluctuating.

As they grew in grace, these men and women discovered that the New Testament's picture of a Christian was a picture of *them*. They realised that *they* had the faith in Christ, the attitude to indwelling sin and the brotherly love which are the Scriptural marks of a genuine believer. It was not a cold deduction, but a conviction which the Holy Spirit rooted within their spirits.

This work of the Holy Spirit, although it accompanied their study of the Scriptures, was nonetheless a direct action of the Spirit within their souls. Now that they no longer have access to the Bible this direct witness does not leave them, because although it accompanied their study of Scripture it was never actually *dependent* on the Scripture (which it would be, of course, if Lutheranism was right). In their cells these martyrs continue to know God as 'Abba, Father' and cry out to Him as such from their hearts, because the Spirit bears witness with their spirit that they are children of God.

Considering this aspect of the Holy Spirit's work, Dr Martyn Lloyd-Jones writes:

'It is He alone who can speak with a final authority which gives me certitude with regard to my being a child of God, a certitude as great, or greater indeed, as my certainty with regard to anything else in life. Such a fact is constantly asserted by the saints throughout the centuries. They declare that the Holy Spirit made them so certain of the reality and presence of the Lord Jesus Christ and His love for them, that they were more certain of that than of any other fact whatsoever.'[17]

And it is the same with us, although we are not worthy to be mentioned on the same page as these brave men and women of God. All of us go many hours every day without any easy access to the Scriptures. Six hours a day, five days a week, the young teenage believer endures mockery in her comprehensive school, and goes home in the evening as convinced as ever that she belongs to Christ. The Christian soldier goes for days on end without a moment to open to his Bible, but bends the knees to Christ every night before getting in to his makeshift bed. The believing wife of a taunting husband can often go weeks without having freedom to meditate the Word, but remains totally sure that she is a child of God. What hope would there be for any of these children of God if separation from the Scriptures meant separation from assurance?

The fact is that, whatever may happen to us, certain things can never be taken away from anyone who has been redeemed by Christ. Assurance is one of them. It can fluctuate, it can become very weak, but it can never totally disappear. This is because we have a new nature—a nature which is born of God. Faith in Christ, revulsion at our indwelling sin, love for your fellow-believers, are all kept alive in our hearts by the

Holy Spirit whom God has given to us. The presence of the Holy Spirit is the proof that we belong to the Lord and that heaven is our home.[18] And, by His direct witness within us, He makes His presence *felt*.

4. The felt presence of Christ

*A sense of the Lord's presence was
everywhere. It pervaded, nay, it created
the spiritual atmosphere. It mattered not
where one went, the consciousness of the
reality and nearness of God followed.*

R.B. JONES[19]

Although modern Christianity does not have a great deal to say about spiritual experience, it is still not unusual for someone to tell us, 'I really felt the Lord's presence in the meeting tonight.' You may even have said it yourself. But what did you mean? And how, precisely, did you discern that the Lord was there?

As we consider this subject we must begin by defining our terms. Let us first of all take the word 'presence'. One of my favourite books is *Collins Plain English Dictionary*. It tells us that 'Your presence somewhere is the fact that you are there.'[20] With that in mind, we can define the felt presence of Christ as 'the awareness that where you are, *He* is.' This is how we shall use the term in this chapter.

We shall approach our subject by means of five questions. But before we do so, we need to be very sure that we have mastered what we discovered in chapter 1, and these four points in particular:

- We are body and soul (spirit).

- Emotions/feelings have their root in the soul.

- The human soul has two parts—the understanding (thoughts) and the will.

- Emotions/feelings are strong movements of the will, as we inwardly say 'Yes!' or 'No!' to the varying thoughts that go through our minds.

What you *feel*, then, is almost entirely governed by the thoughts that are going through your head. This is so very important that I need to write it again: what you *feel* is almost entirely governed by the thoughts that are going through your head. This is the point above all points that we must keep in our minds as we now answer our five questions.

1) Is there any difference between the presence of the Father, the presence of the Son, and the presence of the Holy Spirit?

The straight answer is 'No'. If we said any differently we would be betraying the fact that we do not believe in the doctrine of the Trinity.[21] The Bible's teaching is that there is but one God, but that there are three who are God—the Father, the Son and the Holy Spirit; These three are distinct, and are distinguished from each other by their personal properties (that is, there are things to be said about each of them that cannot be said about the others). Generation is an act of the Father alone. Only the Son can be said to be begotten. Procession can be ascribed only to the Holy Spirit.

Within the Godhead there is a certain definite order. The Father is first, the Son second, and the Holy Spirit third. This does not mean that one has existed before another, for each Person is eternally God. Nor does it mean that one Person is senior, the second lesser, and the third junior—for each Person is God in His own right, and the Persons are equal. It is simply a recognition of the eternal relations which exist between the Persons of the Godhead.

These relations within the Godhead are reflected in the way that God *acts*. Everything that God does springs *from* the Father. He is first. It comes to pass *through* the Son. He is second. And it is brought about *by* the Spirit. He is third. All God's works are works of the three Persons jointly. Yes, whenever God does anything it is the Father who is the Cause, the Son who is the Mediator, and the Holy Spirit who is the One who applies and completes. This is the way God works. And this is still the way He is working when we feel His presence.

So it is that the Scriptures teach us that God, who is invisible, makes Himself known in the Son (John 1:18). To see the Son is to see the Father (John 14:9). The way to come to the Father is to come to His Son; to know the Son is to know the Father (John 14:6–7). If the Spirit comes to us, it is the Son who has come to us (John 16:15–20). When the

Son speaks to us, He does it by means of the Spirit speaking to us (Revelation 2:1–2, 7).

There are countless other Scripture verses that we could look at. The message is always the same: if one Person of the Trinity is dealing with us, all three Persons are dealing with us—*God* is dealing with us! This is always the case. God is certainly three, but He is also most certainly one. You cannot divide the Trinity. The three Persons are distinct, but they are not separable. To feel the presence of Christ, then, is to feel the presence of the Godhead. How amazing is that?

2) What are some of the ways in which people in Scripture were made aware of the presence of Christ?

One way was by theophanies. In Old Testament times God sometimes appeared to people in a visible form, usually that of a man or an angel. Such appearances are known as *theophanies*, (or God-appearances).[22] These pre-incarnate appearances were pledges of the Son's eventual coming among us in human nature. As we read of the three visitors who came to Abraham by the terebinth trees of Mamre, it soon becomes clear that one of the men was God Himself (Genesis 18:1–2, 13–14). The man who Jacob wrestled with was God (Genesis 32:24, 30, see Hosea 12:4–5). Moses saw Him in the burning bush (Exodus 3:1–6). Young Samuel heard Him and felt Him near in his bedroom (1 Samuel 3:1–21). In the same way, when Isaiah saw Jehovah in all His glory and prostrated himself in the presence of His overbearing holiness, it was the Lord Jesus Christ that he saw (compare Isaiah 6:1–13 with John 12:39–41).

Another way, and an obvious one, was by the physical presence of the Lord Jesus Christ during His time on earth. The eternal Son of God became man. For thirty-three years He was, just as He continues to be for ever, God and man in two distinct natures and one person. He took to Himself a real body and a reasoning soul as He was conceived by the Holy Spirit in the womb of the virgin Mary, who gave birth to Him. It was the sinless God-Man whose presence was felt in Bethlehem, Nazareth, Jerusalem and everywhere else that He went. The Man who is God was crucified, buried and resurrected. Thomas worshipped the risen Lord, calling Him 'My Lord and my God' (John 20:28). Two disciples experienced His company as they walked with Him to Emmaus and, as He expounded the Old Testament Scriptures, they felt their hearts burning within them. They certainly had an experience of the felt presence of Christ! (Luke 24:13–35).

In addition, after Christ's ascension, members of the early church felt Christ's presence in the dramatic experiences that they had of the Holy Spirit. On the day of Pentecost the Spirit came to them in a howling wind and forked tongues of fire, causing them to powerfully speak of Christ in languages they had never learned and in public preaching (Acts ch.2). Later on, in a time of urgent united prayer, their meeting place was shaken, they were filled with the Spirit, and once more declared the word of God with boldness (Acts 4:31). There were similarly wonderful displays of the Spirit's power in Cornelius' home (Acts 10:44–48), when a group of religious people in Ephesus finally became true believers (Acts 19:1–7), and when Paul struck blind a sorcerer who was opposing the spread of the gospel (Acts 13:4–12). It was clear to all that those first Christians were not simply advocating a new philosophy or teaching a series of principles. A divine presence was accompanying them.

Not only so, but after His ascension there were those who saw Christ, both physically and in visions. Stephen saw Him as he was being stoned to death (Acts 7:54–60). Paul saw and heard Him as he was converted on the Damascus road (Acts 9:1–9, 1 Corinthians 15:8). He saw and heard Him again in a night vision that he had during a time of intense discouragement in Corinth (Acts 18:9) and again, perhaps physically, after his defence before the supreme Jewish council in Jerusalem (Acts 23:11). Finally, the apostle John saw Him in the prophetic vision that he received one Sunday during his imprisonment on the isle of Patmos (Revelation 1:9–20).

Yes, people have seen Christ and known Him near, but this has not always been in the same way. There were many more theophanies than those we have mentioned. The four Gospels speak in detail of the Lord's physical presence on earth. There are experiences of the Holy Spirit on almost every page of the Acts, and the Epistles and the Revelation speak about other sightings and visions. But we live in the twenty-first century, long after biblical days. What about us? What can *we* expect?

3) Can we expect the Lord to use similar means to make *us* aware of the presence of Christ?

Once more, the answer has to be 'No!' Theophanies are clearly a thing of the past. Since the incarnation of our Lord we no longer have any need of them. Nor do we have to yearn to be transported back to the first century to witness His life and ministry. Everything that we need to know about that period has been faithfully recorded for us by His chosen witnesses and, whenever we want to, we can read it in the Gospels. The longing for His physical presence that *we* have is our looking forward to the Second Coming and to our being 'always ... with the Lord' (1 Thessalonians 4:17).

Even if we cannot be physically present with Christ just yet, can we not have a sighting of Him, such as Stephen had, or a vision? No. Paul, writing under the inspiration of the Holy Spirit, makes it clear that he was the last to see Christ physically (1 Corinthians 15:8). No one has seen Him since. Every claim to have done so is false. It is phoney. Even John on Patmos did not have physical sightings of Christ. The whole book of Revelation is a prophetic vision, and from this nothing must be taken away, just as nothing must be added (Revelation 22:18–19). Nothing!

The normal experience of Christians is summarised for us by Peter in his first epistle, where he writes of 'Jesus Christ, whom having not seen you love'. But this does not mean that we have lost out, for he continues, 'Though now you do not see him, yet believing, you rejoice with joy inexpressible and full of glory, receiving the end of your faith—the salvation of your souls.' (1 Peter 1:7–9). This is the language of high emotion. Our indescribable pleasure and unspeakable joy is in no way linked to our seeing anything, but it *is* linked to our having faith. This is the path that we must pursue.

What the New Testament teaches is clear and plain: spiritual experience is not a matter of the senses, and is especially not a matter of sight. From start to finish the Christian life is a life of faith (2 Corinthians 5:7). But what *is* faith? It is 'the assurance of things hoped for, the conviction of things not seen' (Hebrews 11:1).[23] Faith is being sure of the unseen. It is not being sure of the *unknown*, but of the *unseen*. The Bible tells us that some things are unseen because they have not happened yet, or because we have not yet arrived where they are. God promises them and we see them as realities. Other things are unseen because, by definition, they cannot be seen. This is supremely true of God, but is also true of angels and demons. Believing what God Himself has revealed in His Word, I am sure of their existence and allow this reality to govern all my thoughts, words and actions.

There are, then, two aspects to faith. I am sure of two sorts of unseen reality. My certainty in both cases, however, is built on the same foundation: God has spoken and I believe what He has said. To me these things are matters of fact. They are not less real, but more real! We believers are confident of what we hope for and are convinced of what we do not see.

Any life which is not motivated by faith is, by definition, displeasing to God (see Hebrews 11:5-6). The Christian life is lived in the consciousness that 'the things which are seen are temporary, but the things which are not seen are eternal' (2 Corinthians 4:18). What can be touched, heard, seen, smelt and tasted is only of passing interest to us. All the things which have really captured our hearts cannot be detected by the senses. Our treasure is not on earth, but in heaven (Matthew 6:19–21). The city to which we belong is not on earth and we can't live here as if it were (Hebrews 11:10, 13–16). This means that our minds are not focused on smoking mountains, flashes of lightning, blasting trumpets or even audible voices. We are not interested in phenomena. We are not! For we have 'come to Mount Zion and to the city of the living God, the heavenly Jerusalem, to an innumerable company of angels, to the general assembly and church of the first-born who are registered in heaven, to God the judge of all, to the spirits of just men made perfect, to Jesus the mediator of the new covenant, and to the blood of sprinkling that speaks better things than that of Abel' (Hebrews 12:22–24).

4) How, then, are we normally made aware of the presence of Christ?

The answer to this question does not lie in our experiencing any phenomena, but in something inward. We need to remind ourselves of all that we learned in chapters 1 and 2. We have been born again. We are new creations. We have received a new nature and have been transformed in our very souls. This means, of course, that our understanding and our will have been revolutionised, and that we now have new feelings which unconverted people have never experienced, and which they are not able to experience.

For example, an unconverted person may hear a sermon which explains a passage of the Bible and, in doing so, lifts up the Lord Jesus Christ. The sermon is not mumbo-jumbo to this person. They understand what is being said. But they do not take it to heart. They do not receive it and make it their own. They do not believe what they hear. They are not thrilled by it. They simply do not see the vastness, the glory, the wonder and the eternal significance of the message. They have no desire to remember it and no intention of living by it. And why is this? It is because 'the natural man does not receive the things of the Spirit of God, for they are foolishness to him; nor can he know them, because they are spiritually discerned' (1 Corinthians 2:14).

How different we believers are! We have been renewed in the spirit of our mind (Ephesians 4:23). Because of the work of the Holy Spirit in our heart, we know that we are not being hoodwinked, but that we are hearing the truth (1 John 2:20, 27). And it moves us. Something inside us says 'Yes!' to the message. We understand what we hear, believe it, love it and determine to live by it. As the Lord Jesus Christ is exalted by the preacher, we catch a sight of Him by faith. A fire burns in our heart. We worship Him, love Him, feed on Him and have new desires for Him. We feel that He is dealing with us personally. The preacher's voice fades and it seems to us that it is Christ who is speaking. We feel that He is near. He is *present*!

It is not just our understanding that is affected. The inward 'Yes!' is a strong movement of the will. We are drawn towards what we are hearing. In our souls we move towards it. It is e-motion. But that is not all; we decide, humbly, to work at our Christian lives and to take the action which the preached Scriptures require. This is what always happens when God is at work in a human soul (Philippians 2:12–13). As we have seen, any inward emotion which is not matched by outward obedience is not an emotion on which our Lord smiles.

Deep feeling during and after biblical preaching is a common spiritual experience. But we have other spiritual experiences as well. Sometimes inexplicable things happen to us, but our *thoughts* tell us that they have happened because Christ is with us. The best way of illustrating this is by referring to some biblical examples.

In Genesis chapter 24 we find an unnamed servant of Abraham travelling back to where his master came from in order to find a bride for Isaac, Abraham's son and heir. He arrives at his destination in the evening and waits by the city well, praying that the first young lady who offers to water his camels might be the right wife for Isaac. His prayer is answered at once, and in this way he is led to Rebekah, Abraham's niece, who returns with him to marry Isaac. In narrating the whole event to Laban, Rebekah's brother, the servant makes it clear that he does not see this as a coincidence, but as a providence arranged by the Lord who was with him (see Genesis 24:42–48).

Our lives as believers are filled with 'coincidences'. One Sunday morning when I was preaching I found myself saying some very strong things about the evils of freemasonry. These comments were not in my notes and were completely unplanned. They arose on the spot as a legitimate application of the biblical passage being expounded. At the end of the service a young man, recently converted, approached me. The conversation went like this:

'How did you know?', he said.

'How did I know what?'

'How did you know that my father was in the service this morning?'

'I didn't know, but what exactly is concerning you?'

'You must have known, because of what you said about freemasonry. My father is the leading freemason for the whole of this area and he didn't like what you said. But I am so happy that the preaching has impacted him so strongly'.

All of us have a store of similar stories. I concluded from the young man's comments that the Lord had been with me as I had made those impromptu remarks, and I felt thrilled, privileged and vindicated. But how did I come to my conclusion? It was from the thoughts that went through my mind—thoughts not of 'luck' or 'coincidence', but of the biblical doctrine of providence and the certainty that the Lord 'works all things according to the counsel of his will' (Ephesians 1:11). He had been with me as I preached, and I felt awed.

The freemason was shaken by the preaching but, to my knowledge, was never converted. How different was an art student who, one Sunday evening, walked past the church building. Interested by its architecture, she decided to go in and have a look at the interior. She arrived just as the sermon was beginning, so she sat down respectfully and looked around. But she could not shut out the sermon. The secrets of her heart were revealed, she slumped down in her seat, felt that she was in the presence of God and called out to Christ to be her Saviour and Lord (see 1 Corinthians 14:25). But what made her feel that the Lord was present? She witnessed no signs, wonders, miracles or 'supernatural' phenomena. Something took place in her *thoughts*. Her hidden, intimate, secret thoughts were laid bare by the Word of God. She was brought to feel the presence of God, not by anything *outward*, but by something *inward*.

This is the way it always is. The day came when the apostle Paul had to defend himself before the Emperor Nero. He knew that he would either leave court as a free man or that he would be sentenced to death. As it happened, he did so well in presenting his case that the outcome was referred to a second hearing. Writing of his experience that day, he said, 'The Lord stood with me and strengthened me' (2 Timothy 4:17). Standing in the dock he had felt the presence of Christ!

What was it that led Paul to conclude that the Lord had stood with him? He was not in a meeting with like-minded people, with sweet music playing and a conducive 'atmosphere'. He was in a hostile courtroom with not even a single friend in the public gallery! But as he gave his defence he was aware of a strength that was not his own. Poor though he was as a public speaker (see 2 Corinthians 10:10) the words flowed and flowed, and he was able to give a thorough and comprehensive explanation of the gospel message. The hundreds of non-Jews present heard the only message that could save them. The effect was so stunning that the hearing was adjourned and Paul was alive for a little longer. How could all this be explained? Only one explanation was possible: the Lord Jesus Christ had been present and had preached to them all by means of a human instrument. This was the *thought* that ran through the apostle's mind and which totally convinced him. And the thought provoked a 'Yes!' within his soul and flooded him with emotion. He had *felt* the Lord to be with him.

Feelings are strong movements of the will, as our souls move towards or away from the thoughts in our minds. Sometimes the Holy Spirit plants new thoughts in our minds, which is the explanation for a great deal of our spiritual experience. More often, He stirs us to remember some teaching or promise of Scripture. When we are praying with others we remember the promise of Matthew 18:20 and know and feel the Saviour to be among us. Standing on doorsteps in door-to-door visitation our minds go to Matthew 28:20 and we no longer feel alone. In our dying moments we are invaded by Psalm 23:4 and feel a supernatural peace. It is not mystical. Our mind is not switched off. Our most exalted spiritual experiences are accompanied by our most vigorous and scriptural thinking, and the more robust and theological our thinking is, the more likely we are to experience the felt presence of the Saviour we love.

5) To have a properly balanced view of this subject, what other points should we take on board?

There are at least three. First of all, we must stop identifying the presence of Christ with *places*. Sometimes we hear people say that as soon as they entered a certain place, they were aware of the Lord's presence. This is sheer superstition. 'God, who made the world and everything in it, since he is Lord of heaven and earth, does not dwell in temples made with hands' (Acts 17:24). There is no location in the universe which is holier than another. There are no holy buildings or holy places anywhere. There do not need to be, because 'he is not far from each one of us, for in him we live and move and have our being' (Acts 17:27–28). He can reveal Himself to us at any time, in any place, and in any set of circumstances. The awareness of 'The Universal Presence'[24] is an *inward* experience. It does not depend on anything circumstantial.

During the Welsh Revival of 1903–1905[25] an outstanding meeting took place in Amlwch, Anglesey, during which R.B. Jones preached with unusual power on Isaiah chapter 6. The hearers were crushed by an awareness of God's holiness, by the awfulness of their sin and by a sense of severe impending judgment. Then they broke their hearts with emotion as they heard of God's forgiveness, and of His gracious and complete removal of their vileness. They were beside themselves with heavenly joy. R.B. Jones then records that 'the holy presence of God was so manifested that the speaker himself was overwhelmed; the pulpit where he stood was so filled with the light of God that he had to withdraw!'[26]

What are we to make of this? The Holy Spirit was taking hold of Scriptural truth and enlivening it in an extraordinary way within the minds of those present. As He both changed and revived people's souls, they undoubtedly responded with an inward 'Yes!' of the highest intensity. The meeting was glorious and everyone knew it to be so. The preacher was overwhelmed with the wonder of what he was preaching. All this was inward. His comment about the light of God in the pulpit, however, is out of step with the rest of his narrative. If God does not dwell in man-made temples, He certainly does not dwell in man-made pulpits! R.B. Jones was undoubtedly amazed at what God had given him in that pulpit. He was overcome with awe. The experience was so extraordinary that he probably felt that his human frame could not take any more, so he hastened to leave the pulpit where the experience had been given to him. But we cannot believe that the Shekinah glory of Old Testament days—a picture or 'type' of the coming Christ—was manifested in a Welsh chapel in New Covenant days. This would be a return to the phenomenal, which was a mark of the Old Covenant. We thank the Lord for what He did in Amlwch that night, but consider that R.B. Jones should have been more accurate in the way that he described it.

To have a properly balanced view of our subject we must take to heart a second point. By the inward work of His Spirit, the Lord certainly gives to His people exalted experiences. These are inward, personal, and are not the same for everybody. But they are not to be gloried in. We should only speak about them with restraint. There is something much, much bigger which should be the subject of our glorying.

It is always a mistake to get over excited about our spiritual experiences. The members of the Corinthian church had not grasped this, and so put themselves in spiritual danger. Into their midst came a number of preachers who boasted constantly of all the wonderful experiences that the Lord had given them, and of the extraordinary gifts that He had entrusted them with. The Corinthians were mesmerised by these preachers, began to follow their every directive without question, and then began to despise the apostle Paul. With such wonderful men as their new leaders, how could they go on giving serious attention to a man who did not seem to have any of these wonderful experiences of the supernatural?

What the Corinthians had not realised, however, was that these supposedly wonderful men were actually charlatans who were imposing on the church another gospel, which was not the divinely-revealed gospel at all. They were 'false apostles, deceitful workers, transforming themselves into apostles of Christ' (2 Corinthians 11:13). Led astray by their heroes, the Corinthians were on the point of turning their back on God's saving truth! Paul spends almost all of 2 Corinthians tackling the problem, concluding by relating some of his own spiritual experiences and calling the whole process foolish.

Paul's point is that true spiritual experience does not lead people to think highly of themselves. It brings them to the point where they see that they are utterly weak, that they have no strength of their own, and that any strength that they *do* have has come to them immediately from Christ. True spiritual experience leads believers to think highly of *Him*, and to see everything else in the whole world as of no real importance.

He makes the same point in his epistle to the Galatians. Here, too, professing believers were departing from the gospel. But the problem was not miracle-working pseudo-apostles, but teachers who taught their hearers to rely on Christ *and* rites, ceremonies and good deeds. Inevitably these became the things that they gloried in, to which Paul retorts: 'But God forbid that I should glory except in the cross of our Lord Jesus Christ, by whom the world has been crucified to me, and I to the world' (Galatians 6:14). There is only one thing in the world to be enthused about. It is not our religious practices and it is not our feelings or spiritual experiences, however genuine any of these things may be. It is the message of Christ and His cross. It is the slain Lamb who is the song of heaven, and anything on earth which is heavenly sings about Him too.

The third point to take to heart should now be clear to us. We have seen that the felt presence of Christ is an inward experience brought about by the Holy Spirit as He works in our thought life. We have also seen that what should enthuse us is the cross-centred message of the gospel. It flows from these two points that what goes on in our thoughts is of supreme importance. We should therefore be constantly cultivating holy thoughts. Every day of our lives we should be prayerfully seeking a fuller and better understanding of the Word and ways of God.

When Paul writes to the Christians at Ephesus he not only tells them that he is praying for them, but also reveals exactly what he requests in those prayers. This is spelled out for us in Ephesians 1:15–23. The briefest study of this great paragraph will discover that what Paul wants for these new believers, above everything else, is that they should *understand* something. He tells them that he is praying 'that the God of our Lord Jesus Christ, the Father of glory, may give to you the spirit of wisdom and revelation in the knowledge of him, the eyes of your understanding being enlightened, that you may know ...' (Ephesians 1:17–18). He particularly wants them to grasp what has happened to them and where they are going.

Holy emotions and spiritual experiences come about because of what is going through the believer's mind. 'Mysticism' is the word that we use for spiritual experiences that cannot be understood by reasoning, and true spirituality is not mysticism. The Bible lays great stress on the importance of feeding the mind. This is why Paul writes that in church he would rather speak five words with his understanding, in order to teach others, than utter ten thousand words in a tongue. He then continues, 'Brethren, do not be children in understanding; however, in malice be babes, but in understanding be men' (1 Corinthians 14:19–20).

The human soul is in two parts, the understanding (or thoughts, or mind) and the will. To strengthen the soul you must strengthen the understanding. The clearer the understanding, the more likelihood there is of a decisive 'Yes!' or 'No!' to its thoughts—in other words, the more likelihood there is of a holy and healthy emotional life. On the road to Emmaus it was as they understood the Scriptures that the disciples' hearts burned within them (Luke 24:32). Any 'feltness' that does not spring from God's Word, or from what God's Word approves (see Philippians 4:8–9), must always be suspect.

5. Guidance

*Guidance is a reality intended for, and
promised to, every child of God. Christians
who miss it thereby show only that they
did not seek it as they should.*

−JAMES I. PACKER[27]

Every day of the Christian life is a day of decision making, and most of the time this presents believers with no difficulty at all. As they listen to the Bible being expounded Sunday by Sunday, and as they read it and think about it during the week, they become increasingly clear about the character of the God whom they worship, and about what pleases Him or displeases Him. Not wanting to grieve Him in any way at all, they adjust their daily behaviour accordingly.

They come to see that in God's Word some things are clearly commanded, while others are clearly forbidden. Of course, they understand that they are saved by Christ and not by keeping God's laws. But right is still right. So they give careful attention to every duty that the Scriptures lay upon them, and equally careful attention to every thought and practice that they are told to lay aside. In their heart of hearts they come to love the law of God (see Romans 7:22) and spend more and more time thinking about it (Psalm 119:97). They especially love the Ten Commandments.

Christians who know their Bibles develop a holy mindset, a godly scale of values and a whole set of biblical instincts that see them safely through this life. They don't need guidance about how to be God-glorifying husbands or wives, parents, children, friends or neighbours. The Bible's teaching is clear and they give themselves to living it out in concrete situations. They know what attitudes should be theirs at work or school, how to use their spare time and how to spend their money. They are aware of what their Lord expects of them as church members and as citizens. They set out, in every area of life, to be men, women and young people who love the Lord their God with all their heart, with all their soul, and with all their mind, and who love their neighbours as themselves (Matthew 22:34–40).

Not commanded and not forbidden

Bible loving believers also know that there are a vast number of areas in life on which the Bible does not speak with any clarity. The best known example relates to alcohol. God's Word has a lot to say about the misuse of intoxicating liquids, but contains no commands to drink them and no commands to abstain from them. It is not surprising, then, that Christians have a wide range of views on this subject, just as they do on such questions as participating in sport, watching television, using Facebook or listening to certain sorts of music. In the early church the issues were different. At that time the discussion and disagreements revolved around such things as what days should be observed as holy, and whether meat offered to idols could legitimately be purchased and eaten by those who follow the Lord Jesus Christ. Differences of conscience on matters of Christian liberty are an ever-present aspect of spiritual experience.

Even in these areas the Christian does not need 'guidance'. The Bible has whole chapters on how to handle such matters.[28] In summary, we can say that all believers who ask themselves five questions, and remember five principles, will walk a safe path.

The five questions are these:

1. If I do this, in what ways will I be able to bring glory to God? (1 Corinthians 10:31).

2. Will it help me in my Christian life? (1 Corinthians 10:23).

3. Does this thing have a tendency to enslave those who do it? (1 Corinthians 6:12).

4. Will it strengthen me against temptation? (Matthew 6:13).

5. Will it draw me nearer to the Lord or nearer to the world? (1 John 2:15–17).

As G. Campbell Morgan wrote: 'The things which hinder are not necessarily low or vulgar. They may be in themselves noble things, intellectual things, beautiful things. But if our participation in any of these dims our vision of the ultimate goal in the purpose of God, holds us in our running, makes our going less determined and steady, they become weights and hinder.'[29]

The five principles are these:

1. In areas like this, we must not expect everyone's conscience to agree (Romans chapter 14).

2. Because someone differs from me in an area of conscience, it does not necessarily mean that they are less sincere in following the Lord (Romans 14:6).

3. When we differ about this, we are not to quarrel (Romans 14:1, 10).

4. If I consider that I can do something with a clear conscience, I am still not to do it if it will genuinely hinder a fellow-believer in their spiritual progress (Romans 13:10, 14:13–17, 21).

5. If I have even the slightest doubt about whether I should do it, I should not do it (Romans 14:22–23).

The biblically instructed Christian, of course, will know these things. They will have become part of that set of godly instincts which has built up in their heart over the years. This Christian will also know that any restrictions that they place on their liberty of conscience will be self-imposed. They will be part of their inward life. No fellow believer, church or organisation has any right under Christ to impose any rules about these things on any Christian anywhere. Christ alone is the Lord of conscience.

Vocational choices

On an average day, then, a Bible-loving Christian does not need any 'guidance'. But there is an area in which we all face difficulty. It is the sphere of what James Packer calls 'vocational choices'.[30] A number of doors are open before me and I don't know which one to go through. For example: should I get married, or not? If so, who should I marry? Should I live here, or there, or somewhere else? Of the various job opportunities presenting themselves to me, which one should I take? There are a number of equally good churches in the area, so which one should I join? Is it time for us to have another child? To what causes should I give my money? What specific work to advance the gospel should I be committed to?

These questions, and similar ones, I cannot ignore. I have got to make a decision and I want to make one which will please the Lord. But how, exactly, do I go about it? This is a realm of spiritual experience in which we all need instruction.

The first thing to say is that this is not a time for me to lay aside my Bible. I need the Word of God at this moment as much as I have ever needed it. It may not address my particular problem directly, but it has *something* to say which is relevant to it. It lays down boundaries that will limit my choices. For example, on the marriage question, it tells me that I am free to marry or not to marry, but that I am not free to marry a non-Christian. When it comes to employment choices, I am not free to engage in any profession which is dishonest or immoral, and I should normally expect to work in line with my talents and interests. If I am choosing a new home, I am not free to live beyond my means. If my problem relates to clothing, I must remember that the Lord expects me to dress modestly. When it comes to 'vocational choices', Christians who remain close to their Bibles seldom go astray.

But even with the Bible's limits in mind, my problem is not really solved. Now that the field of legitimate choice is clear to me, I still have to commit myself to one set of responsibilities more than another. What does the Lord want me to do? And how can I know?

It is obvious that I should talk to Him about it, and, if necessary, that I should talk to Him at length. A good place to start would be to talk to Him about what His Word says in Romans 12:1–2:

> 'I beseech you therefore, brethren, by the mercies of God, that you present your bodies a living sacrifice, holy, acceptable to God, which is your reasonable service. And do not be conformed to this world, but be transformed by the renewing of your mind, that you may prove what is that good and acceptable and perfect will of God.'

In His presence I can parade His mercies through my thoughts. I can reflect on all the great themes that Paul has already treated in the first eleven chapters of Romans—I can contemplate the depths of my sin, the wonder of God's grace, the glorious truths of justification, sanctification, adoption, glorification and election. I can ponder them until my heart is once more overwhelmed by all that the Lord has done for me. And then I can respond to those mercies by telling the

Lord how much I love Him, and how in body and mind I want to be His, and His only, and that I have no desire except to do His will and to prove it to be good, acceptable and perfect. Is it possible that a loving Heavenly Father would let such of child of His go astray?

Or I can reverently but boldly remind the Lord of some of His promises regarding guidance and then make a biblical prayer for guidance my own. The promises I plead might include such verses as these:

'I will instruct you and teach you in the way you should go; I will guide you with my eye' (Psalm 32:8).

'Good and upright is the Lord; therefore he teaches sinners in the way. The humble he guides in justice, and the humble he teaches his way ... Who is the man that fears the Lord? Him shall he teach in the way he chooses' (Psalm 25:8–9, 12).

'The Lord will guide you continually' (Isaiah 58:11).

'Trust in the Lord with all your heart, and lean not on your own understanding; in all your ways acknowledge him, and he shall direct your paths' (Proverbs 3:5–6).

Biblical prayers that I can make my own might be these:

'Show me your ways, O Lord; teach me your paths. Lead me in your truth and teach me. For you are the God of my salvation; on you I wait all the day' (Psalm 25:4–5).

'Teach me your way, O Lord, and lead me in a smooth path, because of my enemies' (Psalm 27:11. See 86:11).

'Teach me to do your will, for you are my God; your Spirit is good. Lead me in the land of uprightness' (Psalm 143:10).

In addition to rededicating myself to the Lord, and to pleading His promises and using biblical prayers, I can (and should) also go to the Lord with James 1:5–8:

'If any of you lacks wisdom, let him ask of God, who gives to all liberally and without reproach, and it will be given to him. But let him ask in faith, with no doubting, for he who doubts is like a wave of the sea driven and tossed by the wind. For let not that man suppose that he will receive anything from the Lord; he is a double-minded man, unstable in all his ways.'

I can tell the Lord about my dilemma. I can remind Him that He is wise and that I am not, and I can ask Him to enlighten me and to give me His wisdom as I make the decision in front of me. And then, in faith, I must wait for the answer.

In all these cases, however, what I must *not* do is to tell the Lord exactly how He must answer my prayer! In chapter 2 of this book we learned about the work of the Holy Spirit in the soul. We saw that the Spirit deals with us immediately and directly. He works in our souls from within. He is well able to remind me of something in His Word which will fully solve my problem, and often that is all that is needed. But He is equally able to plant a completely new thought in my head, and this may be the way that my prayer is answered. Or I may receive a 'prompting', as some people call it—that is, a deep, settled and growing conviction that a certain course of action is the right one. This conviction becomes 'bigger than I am', as we say, and brings me to the point where I feel inwardly compelled to go in a certain direction, and have no ease or peace of conscience as I consider other possibilities.

That is not all. In His providence, the Lord may intervene in my situation in such a way that all the open doors shut, except for one, making it obvious which door I should go through. Or something quite exceptional and unexpected may occur. We saw in chapter 4 that, as New Testament believers, we have no real interest in phenomena. Walking by faith as we do, it would be completely out of character for us to ask God for any form of guidance which might appeal to one of the five senses. But that does not rule out the possibility that God, in His wisdom, and for reasons known only to Him, may choose to act in this way. Our part is to ask God to guide us and to believe that He will. His part is to answer us exactly as He pleases. We ask for guidance, and that is all. Poor creatures that we are, it would be the height of arrogance to dictate to the Almighty and all-wise God as to how He should do this.

Biblical reminders, new thoughts, inward compulsions, providential interventions or the completely unexpected— these are some of the means which the Lord may use to guide us, and we will give some examples of them in a moment.

The important thing to stress, however, is that there is such a thing as waiting on God, as literally dozens of Scripture verses remind us. To 'wait on the Lord' means to have powerful, personal, sustained dealings with Him. He will not guide us if we keep our distance from Him. He will not allow us to walk on His road unless we do so in complete dependence on Him. He is not in a hurry and, if we want to walk life's journey with Him, we must learn to walk at His speed. He will often keep us waiting. He seldom, if ever, sheds light on more than the next step, or a few paces ahead. But those who discover the joys of intimacy with Him will recognise His guidance in whatever ways He cares to give it to them.

Biblical reminders

This said, and without pretending that the list is exhaustive, let us now have some examples of the different ways in which the Lord may guide us in our 'vocational choices'. I have presented them as five categories but, as we shall see, it is not as simple as that. Sometimes they overlap, so that it is not clear into which category some experiences fit.

In giving these examples I shall sometimes refer to what has happened to others, but please forgive me for telling you about a number of my own experiences as well. I want to write to you with feeling, but also to underline that personal dealings with God are not a thing of the past. He still guides His children today.

Sometimes, when we simply do not know what to do, the Lord brings to our mind a passage or teaching of Scripture which we have completely forgotten. This should not surprise us. The Lord wants us to know everything in His Word and to mentally engage with it. As we have seen, this is His normal way of steering us safely through this life. But we are sinful, weak and forgetful; it is simply impossible for us to remember everything that He has revealed. So, by a wonderful action of His Spirit in our soul, He brings it back to our mind.

On the evening before His crucifixion, Our Lord spent time with His disciples and had a great deal to tell them. But how were they going to remember it all? And decades later, how did the apostle John manage to record everything Jesus said that evening *word for word*? The answer is found in our Lord's words in John 14:26: 'But the Helper, the Holy Spirit, whom the Father will send in my name, he will teach you all things, and bring to your remembrance all things that I said to you.'

This is a promise made specifically to those early disciples and it does not apply to us in the same way. But it does shed light on a common spiritual experience. How is a saved sinner, who has completely forgotten large parts of God's Word, suddenly able to recall just the passage that he needs, and very often able to do it in the exact words of Scripture? It is obviously because of a work of the Holy Spirit in their soul.

Although I have spent the greater part of my life in preparing sermons and preaching them, I have spent almost as many hours in what today is called 'counselling'. As a minister of the gospel, I believe that my practice in one-to-one encounters with needy people should be basically the same as my practice in the pulpit: my calling is to explain and apply the Word of God. How thankful I am, then, for the biblical reminders that the Spirit brings to the mind!

When someone comes to see me, I ask them to tell me about their problem. I let them talk and talk until they have told me their story three times, and I do not normally interrupt them except to ask them to clarify certain points. In nearly all cases I have no idea how I am going to advise them at the end. I am completely stumped. So, as they continue talking, I pray that the Lord will have mercy on them by guiding my thoughts and words, and by giving me wisdom in what to say. And, in fifty years of counselling, nobody has ever left without some clear word of direction.

As they speak and I pray, I find that without fail parts of Scripture spring to my mind, and often they are parts that I have not read recently and have largely forgotten. My responsibility now is to explain the Scriptures' teaching and to apply it to their situation. Maybe a doctrine has to be taught, a duty underlined, a fear quelled or an encouragement given. All I can say is that it has been my immense privilege to see countless lives changed for ever because of the way that their problems have been seen and addressed in the light of God's Word. What a glorious experience this is!

It is not only in counselling that I have experienced this aspect of the Spirit's work. For example, once at a communion service a man came in who was under discipline from his church, a fact that was known by most people present. As he sat down he appeared hostile and aggressive, but when he took the communion bread hardly anyone noticed. Things were very different when the communion cups came round; he made a scene and snatched a cup from the serving deacon. What was I, as the presiding minister, to do?

At that moment my eye fell on a verse in the Book of Proverbs which, for some reason, I had open in front of me. With an unusual authority I found myself saying, 'They eat the bread of wickedness, and drink the wine of violence'[31] (Proverbs 4:17). The effect on the congregation was startling. There was a sudden and total silence. There was also a tangible sense of relief, because the church felt that its discipline had been maintained, that the man concerned had been shown up by Scripture itself, and that the Holy Spirit had been at work.

Something more comforting, but of the same order, happened during the early years of the ministry of Howell Harris.[32] After many inward struggles and much praying, Harris had come to Christ on Whitsunday, 1735. He began to live a new life, but it was not all plain sailing, because one moment he was bathing in the peace of forgiveness and the next moment he was strongly tempted to atheism. His soul was ablaze with love for God and the resolve to never displease Him, and yet the slightest failure made him feel that he had fallen from grace and had lost his salvation. His inward conflicts and contradictions were so strong that he was even tempted to commit suicide.

We read that 'in the fury of the storm the words, "I, the Lord, change not," shot into his mind with such power that the turbulent sea within him was quieted. He had never heard before this word of Scripture, but to his dying day he loved it more than any other word. In the darkest periods, when every star was obscured and all hope had vanished, his soul clung to this verse. This was his sure anchor, and it kept its hold a thousand times after all else had given way. This verse brought him to "the glorious liberty of the children of God" and to realise that what alone mattered was God's mighty grasp of him.'[33]

New thoughts

How shall we define Harris's experience? A verse of Scripture came to his mind and kept him from choosing a wrong path. But we can hardly call it a biblical *reminder*, because he had never heard the verse before. A new thought had come into his mind, a thought that he had never had previously; but in this case the new thought was expressed in the very words of inspired Scripture.

How is such a thing possible? We are in no difficulty here if we have taken to heart what we learnt earlier in this book. The human soul is composed of two parts, the thoughts (or understanding) and the will. The Holy Spirit works *within* the soul, and gives to its active powers a totally new direction. Being God, the Spirit is well able to sow totally new thoughts within the human mind, and, if He pleases, He can easily do this in the very words of the Scriptures that He has breathed out.

Howell Harris had had a similar experience in the weeks before his conversion. While he was praying in the belfry of Llangasty church, the thought came strongly into his mind that he should give himself to God, although he had never heard of such a thing, and had no idea how to do it, or why.

All he knew was that with the thought came a comfortable willingness to pursue the idea.[34] And a few months later, after his conversion, we find him preaching Christ to all and sundry without having any idea beforehand of what he was going to say. Thoughts, old *and new*, poured into his mind, allowing him to speak with power for two, three, or even four hours at a time.[35] What was this, if it was not an example of the Holy Spirit's work, directing him into his life's work?

All Christians who engage in any form of witness to Christ know something of this experience. Face to face with mockers and opponents, they often have no idea of what they should say. Then, 'from nowhere', comes a sentence or two that is so right, so apposite, so powerful and so convincing, that their tormenters are stunned and baffled, and having nothing more to say.

All of us who are engaged in advising others enjoy this experience on a regular basis. It is not just Scripture that comes into our mind. One example will explain what I mean. A young Christian couple, anguished by their marital difficulties, once came to me for help. Their problem was complex and the only way to help them was to find an older couple who had expertise in two distinct areas. Not only so, but these older people would need to be believers who could keep a secret and who would be willing to invest time and energy in two young people in distress. But where could such a couple be found?

I told the young couple that I would find an older couple to help them and that I would be back in touch in a few days time. Within a few hours I was regretting saying such a thing. The fact is that I did not know of anyone anywhere who could help them. Name after name raced through my mind, but no one that I knew was suitable.

Everything changed in the secret place. As I laid the whole situation before the Lord, I suddenly found myself thinking about a couple I had known years ago and whom I had only seen on rare occasions since. I thought about what sort of people they were, the experiences they had had in life, the expertise they had acquired through the years, and their present geographical location. They were tailor-made for the situation—a perfect match! What a privilege it was to put the younger couple in touch with them. But where had the thought come from?

Inward compulsions

Just as the Holy Spirit can bring new thoughts into our souls, He can also touch our wills. A certain course of action suggests itself powerfully to our mind, and we find ourselves inwardly compelled to say 'Yes!' to it. The whole idea becomes stronger than we are. We sense that we can't resist, although sometimes we begin by fighting against it until we are eventually conquered. We come to the point where we feel that to choose any other path would compromise our conscience and displease our Lord. We warm to the idea and, despite our fears and doubts, find that the contemplated course of action both attracts and thrills us.

It is precisely because there is such an experience as this that so many of us find ourselves in the Christian ministry, go abroad as missionaries, or serve the Lord in countless other ways, whether 'full-time' or not. I have never really been happy about the expressions 'a call to the ministry' and 'a call to the mission field', because they are so open to misunderstanding. The fact is, however, whether I like the expressions or not, there is such a thing and this is what it is. And woe to those who proceed along those paths without it! No one can survive in Christian work who lacks the inward conviction that the Risen Lord Himself has sent them to their particular field of service.

However, we must be careful. Despite the fact that the Lord has given every believer a new heart, many left-overs of our old nature remain within each one of us. We can easily deceive ourselves into thinking that the Lord is sending us somewhere, or telling us to do some particular task, when nothing of the sort is happening at all. Nor must we ever put inward compulsions on the same level as Scripture. To disobey the Word of God is always sin. But it is not sin to disobey an inward constraint. It can never carry the same authority as the inerrant, written Word. That Word applies to the whole of humanity the whole of the time, whereas an inward compulsion applies only to one person, and at a particular time. Disobeying an inner constraint only becomes sinful when that constraint has taken hold of us so deeply that it has become an issue of conscience.—and we have seen earlier in this chapter, albeit briefly, how issues of conscience are to be handled.

The only safe way to proceed with a 'prompting' is to reflect on it in the presence of God. We ask our heavenly Father to show us if this idea is in any way at odds with Scripture. We pray for wisdom. We surrender to the Lord and tell Him that we only want to do His will, and never our own. We ask Him to confirm the idea in our heart, if it is truly from Him. We pray the biblical prayers and appeal to the biblical promises that we have already mentioned. And, where appropriate, we consult with spiritually-minded people, and seek to do as much as possible in fellowship with the local church of which we are members.

But we would be foolish to deny that inward compulsions exist. If we do that, we will never be able to understand the history of the Christian church. It was because of inward compulsions that Polycarp travelled to Rome in an attempt to reconcile Christians who differed; that Telemachus died while throwing himself between two gladiators, thus ending such spectacles for ever; that Augustine of Hippo wrote his marvellous books; that Patrick evangelised the Irish; that Wycliffe translated the Bible into English; that Luther nailed his ninety-five theses to the door of the Castle Church in Wittenberg; that Tyndale translated and distributed the New Testament; that Farel exhorted Calvin to remain in Geneva; that John Bunyan began to preach and write; that the first Methodists proclaimed Christ on both sides of the Atlantic; that Spurgeon set out to publish his sermons; that Hudson Taylor went to China; and that Dr Martyn Lloyd-Jones gave up a distinguished medical career to devote himself to preaching the gospel. All these acts, and millions more, we rightly ascribe to the ministry of the Holy Spirit. But He brought them about by inwardly moving people to do them.

Providential interventions

Interwoven with all that we have already explored are what we call 'providential interventions'. God has an eternal purpose which He is bringing to fruition through every single thing that happens in His universe. There is no such thing as 'chance' or 'luck' or 'a coincidence'. Without in any way being responsible for sin, or making His creatures into robots, God is working out His purpose in every event, however small or ordinary. The Bible shows us that every change in the weather, the random shooting of an arrow, the chewing of a worm, the falling of a hair, the flight path of a sparrow, and every decision of every person (even evil ones)—all of these are directed by a sovereign God who is holy, good, wise and powerful. Nothing is out of His control.

It is not surprising, therefore, that it is by providential interventions that God often makes His will known to us. He arranges events in such a way that there is no doubt about which way He wants us to go. A good example of this is seen in the life of the young Spurgeon who, as a teenage pastor, was ready to follow his father's advice and to better himself by studying at a theological college, despite having strong personal doubts about the wisdom of such a course.

It was arranged that Spurgeon should have an initial meeting with the college's principal, and that this should take place at a home in Cambridge. He arrived at the appointed hour and was shown by a maid into a sitting room, where he duly waited for the principal. After two hours of waiting he called for the maid, only to be told that the principal had been waiting in another room and had just left to catch a train! The outcome was that Spurgeon never went to college, and this was one of the facts that commended him to the officers of New Park Street Baptist Church, London (later to become The Metropolitan Tabernacle) where he became the pastor at nineteen years old, and where he spent the rest of his life. The church officers were tired of the boring and unctionless sermons preached by visiting theological students, and were pleased to have a man who preached with unsurpassed knowledge, authority and freshness.[36]

In the late 1970s I was approached by Christians working in Pakistan with a view to helping them provide theological education for the many national pastors of the country. Having had my earliest years in what was then North-West India, I was very attracted to the idea, but I had to think through my responsibilities to my wife and family, and to the church where I was pastor. After weeks of prayer, and of discussion with Doll, I still did not know how I should reply to the invitation. Then a phone call informed me that a Christian leader from Pakistan would be visiting me on a certain Tuesday, and that he would be asking me for my final decision.

On Monday evening the phone rang again. It was a boy in his early teens whom I had known since he was small. He was ringing from the flat where he lived with his mother and stepfather, to tell me that they were engaged in a violent fight and that he was in danger and was frightened. The danger was real, as I found out forty-five minutes later when I carried the boy out of the flat where the arguing and fighting continued. With the possibility that this boy would join our family on a permanent basis (which is what subsequently happened) I knew that there was no likelihood in the foreseeable future of our uprooting ourselves and moving abroad. Our prayer for guidance had been answered in the clearest manner possible. The Lord had chosen to do it by means of a providential intervention.

The completely unexpected—and unsought

Guidance, then, is a reality of Christian experience. As we have stressed earlier, our part is to ask God to guide us and to believe that He will. His part is to answer us exactly as He pleases. He may do this in any of the ways that we have mentioned so far, or in any combination of those ways. Or He may do it in ways which are completely unexpected and unusual. It is up to Him. What we must underline again and again is that it is never right for us to tell the Lord *how* He must do what He has promised to do.

There came a time when Paul and his missionary team did not know what to do. Having preached the gospel in what is now central Turkey, the Lord made it impossible for them to preach in the west, north or north-west. So they found themselves beside the Aegean Sea in the port of Troas, no doubt wondering what the Lord had in store for them. It was there that Paul had a dream, which he shared next morning with his colleagues. On considering it together, they all came to the conclusion that the Lord was calling them to cross the Sea and to proclaim the gospel in Macedonia. The gospel came to Europe because of a dream![37]

Yes, God can guide people through dreams. What we should notice, however, is that Paul did not seek this method of guidance. Nor did he act without consulting others about it and submitting himself to their communal wisdom. In other words, he was very cautious about accepting a dream as a means of guidance, just as we should be.

We should be equally cautious about other means of guidance, but this does not mean that we should discount them out of hand. For example, as Spurgeon reflected on the providence that kept him from meeting the college principal, he 'heard' in his mind a voice that was as forceful as any spoken voice. It said to him, 'Seekest thou great things for thyself? Seek them not!'[38] The voice filled him with joy and confirmed his resolve not to go to college—a course of action which would debar him from any hope of commanding widespread respect, but which resulted in his giving himself even more fully to private study and to humble dependence on the Lord. The 'voice' that he heard that afternoon shaped the whole of his subsequent life and ministry.

Others, without even thinking about such a possibility, have heard a spoken voice. Such was the case with Elwyn Davies who, under God's blessing and in fellowship with others, is the reason why theological liberalism did not kill off authentic biblical Christianity in Wales. As an unconverted theological student, he was once cycling home after spending his day going from door to door to collect clothes to send to the suffering people of war-ravaged Germany. Before reaching Caernarfon, where he was living, a voice asked him, 'Why are you doing this work?' He was all alone and understood at once that the Lord was having dealings with him. Convicted of his own sin and pride, of the emptiness of his religion, and of his need of salvation, he was converted shortly afterwards and gave his life to the defence and proclamation of the gospel. A spoken voice on a lonely country road put him on a higher and better road for the rest of his life.[39]

Who can tell how God may next guide us? None of us can say. But I need to say that there are some ways which the Lord does *not* use in showing us His way. For example, we can completely ignore those who come up to us and say, 'I have a word from the Lord for you', or who use some less subtle way of telling us that they have the gift of prophecy. Such a gift certainly existed in the Old Testament and in the early church. But it does not exist now, despite what many people say. I can defend this statement biblically, but it would take another book to do it! Suffice it to say that my conviction on this point is that of the historic Protestant faith and that there are already plenty of good books available which tackle this subject biblically and in depth.[40] But, as a pastor who cares for people's souls, it is important for me that sincere believers who are earnestly seeking God's will should not be bullied or intimidated by those who do not have their spiritual welfare at heart. When somebody else claims that they know the Lord's will for you, the safe thing to do is to turn and walk away—unless, of course, like Calvin listening to Farel (who did not claim to have a word from the Lord) the words of another stir up a compulsion which is already growing in your own heart.

This has been rather a long chapter, and it has still not said everything that needs to be said about guidance. But hopefully it has made the essential point clear: our Heavenly Father is good and has no intention of misleading any of His children. Those who feed their minds on His Word, patiently wait on Him in prayer and sincerely desire to spend their lives pleasing Him, will not be left in the dark about which way He wants them to go.

6. Asking and receiving

Now this is the confidence that we have in him, that if we ask anything according to his will, he hears us. And if we know that he hears us, whatever we ask, we know that we have the petitions that we have asked of him.

(1 John 5:14–15)

It is well over 1,900 years since the apostle John penned these words, but through the centuries the vast majority of Christians have not taken his statements seriously. It is time to put that right.

Let us be clear about what John is saying. Having just mentioned the Son of God, he tells us that if we are in union with Him, there is something of which we may be sure. It is this: if we ask Him for anything which is in line with His will, whatever it may be, He will listen to our request and will act on it. This being so, we can be certain of receiving what we ask for.

John then applies this wonderful promise to a particular situation, as we see in verses 16–17. Among those who are known as our brothers and sisters in Christ are some who have sinned so significantly that they have, in effect, walked out on the Christian faith. This would include, for example, those who have been excommunicated from gospel churches because of their refusal to repent of their immorality or heretical teaching. They have chosen darkness rather than light. John tells us that we have no obligation to pray for such people. We may do so if we wish, but we must understand that there is no guarantee that our prayers for these people will be answered.

There are others, however, who have not gone as far as that. Because of their sins they are not walking with the Lord very closely, but they have not walked out on Him. If we pray for them, they will be restored. They will be rescued from walking the way of spiritual death and will come back to life. We can have that assurance before their restoration actually takes place.

And that is the whole point. When we pray in line with the Lord's will, we can be sure of having what we ask for, even before it happens! How amazing! This is an experience which every believer can enjoy. It is for every one of us who makes requests 'according to his will'. We can know the outcome of certain events before they actually take place!

This is not the only place where John gives us such teaching. It is found on several occasions in his Gospel, although there he expresses it in different words. Instead of talking about praying 'according to his will', he quotes the promises of our Lord where He instructs us to pray *in his name*. Here are two examples:

'And whatever you ask in my name, that I will do, that the Father may be glorified in the Son. If you ask anything in my name, I will do it' (John 14:13–14).

'And in that day you will ask me nothing. Most assuredly, I say to you, whatever you ask the Father in my name he will give you. Until now you have asked nothing in my name. Ask, and you will receive, that your joy may be full' (John 16:23–24).

Asking 'according to his will' and 'in Christ's name' are the same thing, as a few moments reflection will reveal. When I was ten years old, we lived near a mill where fresh bread was baked and sold every day. Two or three times a week my mother would send me there to buy as many loaves as our family needed. She would tell me exactly what she wanted, and I all I had to do was to remember to ask *according to her will*. But those were not the words I used as I stood at the counter. I would say to the baker, 'Mum says could she have one small brown and two large whites, please.' I would make my request *in her name*. And, without fail, I received what I asked for—as I knew I would!

Misunderstood teaching

The fact that asking 'according to his will' and asking 'in his name' are the same thing has largely been forgotten, and we are all the poorer as a result. In fact, in most Evangelical circles these expressions are spoken about as if they were two separate things.

What sort of prayers are prayed in the average prayer meeting today? A request is made for God to bless next

Sunday's preaching, or for Him to heal a church member who is unwell, 'if it is your will'. The person who is praying does not know whether it is the Lord's will or not, and prays accordingly. He or she simply hopes that it might be and, if it is, that the Lord will hear and act. They do not expect to have any assurance of receiving their petitions until *after* the event. If the preaching is blessed, or the member is healed, they assume that they must have been praying according to the Lord's will. If the preaching is not blessed, or the member is not healed, they assume that they must *not* have been praying according to the Lord's will.

And how is the expression 'praying in his name' understood by most of us? This is usually assumed to be a reference to the mediation of Christ. God is holy, but I am not. How then can I be sure that he will receive both me and my prayer? I trust in the fact that Christ died for my sins and that his perfect righteousness has been put to my account. My sole hope of being heard depends not on myself, but on the atonement of Christ and on his present intercession for me. So I present my prayer 'in his name'.

It is certainly true that all my hopes of being received by a holy God depend on the work of Christ and that I consciously depend on Him as I pray. But this is not what it means to pray 'in his name', as the verses we have quoted from John's Gospel make clear. No! To pray 'in his name' and to pray 'according to his will' are one and the same thing.

If it is only *after* the event that we can know whether we have prayed 'according to his will' or not, the promise of

1 John 5:14–15 is not a promise at all! What the apostle is in fact saying is something very different and truly wonderful. He is telling us to make sure that our petitions are in line with the Lord's will *as we pray*. If we do that, we can pray with total confidence that we are being heard and that our petitions are going to be granted. Where that happens, the place of prayer is no longer a place of uncertainty, but rather of excitement, of expectancy and of fervent praise!

Knowing His will

How then, in prayer, can we know whether our petitions are in line with His will or not? This question is the crux of this chapter. Knowing the answer to it will usher us into realms of spiritual experience of which we may know nothing at the moment.

How can we know the will of God? If we have read and digested the previous chapter, we know the answer. God reveals His will to us in the infallible Scriptures which he has inspired. It follows, then, that if we pray as the Bible instructs us to pray, we can be sure that the Lord will answer us favourably.

For example, in the Lord's Prayer we are told to pray, 'Your kingdom come'.[41] This is not a command to pray for China, America or South Africa, for there are no such commands anywhere in God's Word. It is a command to pray, 'that Satan's kingdom may be destroyed; and that the kingdom of grace may be advanced, ourselves and others brought into it, and kept in it; and that the kingdom of glory may be hastened'.[42] That is as specific as we can make it. But it is in answer to this general request, voiced by millions of believers every day, that the Lord ensures that the gospel continues to make progress throughout the world.

In the secret place, however, general prayers are not enough. I am a preacher, so I ask the Lord to show me what I should preach on and exactly what I should say. Not only so, but what does He want to happen when that particular message is given? What is His will on this specific occasion? These things I need to know, and so I wait on Him until I have the answer. I give myself to prayer before I engage in the ministry of the Word.[43]

We are not all preachers, but all of us who are true Christians are engaged in trying to win others to Christ. We will fail miserably if we try to win everybody, and so we wisely set out to win specific people. But who should they be? So we wait on the Lord and seek His face until He lays particular people, or particular groups of people, on our hearts.

Not only so, but all of us who are committed Christians are members of Bible-believing, Christ-loving, cross-preaching churches. Our churches are of different sizes and are found in vastly differing situations. How shall we pray for our churches? Shall we just pray in a general way, or are there requests specific to *our* church that we should make? If so, what are they? So we wait on the Lord and seek His face, and find ourselves praying with liberty about some subjects, but not being able to pray in the same way about others.

These are only three examples of our need to know the will of God *as we pray*. But that is precisely what

1 John 5:14–15 is about. And when we know His will, and pray for what *He* wants, 'we know that we have the petitions that we have asked of him'.

It is essential, therefore, that a major part of our prayer life should be that of waiting on the Lord until He reveals to us what we should ask. We cannot hurry. We commune with Him until, by His guidance, our requests take shape. This may take a considerable time. However, even then we do not always know 'what we should pray for as we ought, but the Spirit himself makes intercession for us with groaning which cannot be uttered'.[44] In our minds we look at the person, situation or event that we are praying for, but our prayers are not always expressed in any coherent way—we long, and groan, and weep, and yearn. No matter; the Lord reads our hearts and we come into the assurance that we will be heard favourably.

God guides us in prayer just as He guides us in all the other decisions of life. We have covered this in our previous chapter. Our part is to ask Him for guidance, and that is all. His part is make His will clear to us. And He does— eventually! The Lord does things in His own time, but He does not play games with us. He is, after all, our Heavenly Father, and we are His precious children. As we wait on Him, He makes His way plain to us. He does this by any means which He sees appropriate and, as we have said before, it is not for us to dictate to Him how He must act. Biblical reminders, new thoughts, inward compulsions, providential interventions, or by means completely unexpected and unsought—all of these are still used by Him to bring us to the point of praying 'according to his will' and 'in his name'.

The assurance that we have been heard does two things for us. First of all it fills us with expectancy and joy. We look forward with excitement to seeing the Lord work in the way that we know He will. Our confidence in Him has been wonderfully strengthened and our hearts go out to Him in praise as we see His invisible hand at work.

Secondly, our prior assurance of answered prayer helps us to prepare for the situation or event which the Lord is going to bring about. This is very necessary. Knowing that a backslider is going to be restored, we have time to think through how we are going to encourage them in their renewed walk with the Lord. Knowing that a sermon is going to be blessed, we prepare ourselves against the temptation to pride which is inevitably going to follow. Knowing that a church is going to receive new converts, we take steps to advise the existing members on how to deal with the baggage and problems that newly-born brothers and sisters in Christ are certainly going to bring with them.

At this point there is a question which will certainly come to mind: should I tell others about the assurance that I have received in prayer? Speaking for myself, my practice has always been to keep my assurance as a secret between the Lord and myself. This is almost exactly the counsel given by J. Elwyn Davies:

> 'We all know how we can persuade ourselves that he has heard us—particularly when we are praying for the restoration to health of ourselves or of others and for similar serious matters—only for this not to be true. Rather than bringing dishonour upon God's name and the Scriptures, it is better to be careful

and to refrain from telling others about our expectations (other than our closest friends) until those expectations have been fulfilled. Then to bear witness for his glory.'45

Personal experiences

My first experience of 'the prayer of faith', as some people call it, came during my first year as a theological student. During that year I was the member of a team of students who spent every Sunday morning on the surgical ward of a children's hospital, where we ran a Sunday school. On one particular Sunday, just a few minutes before the team was due to leave our college, I felt suddenly ill and went to bed. About thirty minutes or so later, when it was too late to catch the team up, I felt totally well again. At the same time my spirit was invaded by an overwhelming desire to pray.

As you would expect, I prayed with some fervency for the Sunday school in the hospital and for each member of the team. But then my thoughts went to a teenager whom I had met on a beach mission during the previous summer. He had Christian parents who were desperately worried about him because, despite his mild temperament, he did not appear to show any interest at all in spiritual things. With an intensity that I had seldom known before, I found myself praying for his conversion.

My praying for this young man continued through much of the morning, and then, in a way which I cannot really describe, I *knew* that I did not need to pray for his conversion any longer. I got up from my knees weary, and yet exhilarated. There was no doubt in my mind that the young man had been converted. And within a few hours I was in his house, hearing him describe what had happened to him, and sharing the joy of his tearful parents that their son had come to the Lord that very day.

It is over fifty years since that memorable Sunday and I have been favoured with regular experiences of 'the prayer of faith' ever since, especially in sermon preparation. Again and again I have known how a message would 'go' a day or more before preaching it. It happened once more just a couple of weeks ago. In the secret place I received the conviction that the message would move and thrill the people, but that the children's address would do more than that. It would leave both children and adults silenced, instructed and awed. You can imagine with what expectancy I went to the service, and what a privilege it was to see every expectation fulfilled.

The experiences of others

Although through the centuries praying 'according to his will' and praying 'in the name' is an experience that very few believers have known about, there has always been a trickle of men and women who have entered into this open secret. For example, David Martin M'Intyre (1859–1938), author of *The Hidden Life of Prayer*, wrote:

> 'When we pray for temporal blessings, we are sometimes conscious of the special aid of the Spirit of intercession. This is, so far, a warrant to believe that our prayer is well-pleasing to God. But we must be careful not to confound the yearnings of nature with the promptings of the Spirit. Only those who eye is single, and whose whole body,

therefore, is full of light, can safely distinguish between the impulses of the flesh and of the Spirit. Subject to this caution we may very often derive encouragement from the fervour of our petitions.'[46]

In a similar vein, Augustus Toplady (1740–1778) wrote:

'I can, to the best of my remembrance and belief, truly say that I never yet have had one promise, nor assurance, concerning temporal things, impressed upon me beforehand in a way of communion with God, which the event did not realize. I never, that I know of, knew it fail in any one single instance.'[47]

On Tuesday 23rd July 1839 a wonderful revival broke out in the small Scottish town of Kilsyth. The means that God used to bring this about was the preaching of William Chalmers Burns (1815–1886), the son of the local minister, who was then only a young man of twenty-four years old. Within a few days he was preaching for hours at a time to crowds as large as 10,000 people. People were converted in great numbers and it became a common sight to see hundreds of them meeting in the market square so that they could pray together in the morning before going off to work.

Reflecting on the beginning of that great work of the Spirit, which also spread to other parts of Scotland, William Burns (the father) wrote:

'I have since heard that some of the people of God in Kilsyth, who had been longing and wrestling for a time of refreshing from the Lord's presence, and who had, during much of the previous night, been travailing in birth for souls, came to the meeting, not only with the hope, but with well-nigh the certain anticipation of God's glorious appearing, from the impressions they had upon their own souls of Jehovah's approaching glory and majesty.'[48]

This was an identical experience to that which John Livingstone had as he prayed through the night before preaching at Kirk O'Shotts, also in Scotland, on 21st June 1630. The effect of his sermon was extraordinary and over 500 of his hearers were converted and soon joined gospel-loving churches. 'Praying through' or 'praying the prayer of faith' or being 'given assurance' in prayer were expressions which were well understood by some previous generations, but which have virtually descended into oblivion today.[49]

We must stress, however, that the experience to which these expressions refer is not restricted to times of revival. For example, shortly after marrying in China in 1888, missionaries Charles and Priscilla Studd found themselves short of money.[50] They resolved, therefore, that they would ask the Lord to supply their need and so planned to spend the night in prayer. Within twenty minutes of getting on their knees both of them knew that there was no need to pray any longer. There was such a sense of release and relief in their spirits that they knew that the Lord had heard their prayer.

It was almost two weeks before the postman came, but he did not take out of his bag any letter containing money.

C. T. Studd therefore turned the postman's bag upside-down, so sure was he that his prayer had been answered nearly a fortnight earlier. A letter fell to the floor, containing both a cheque and an explanation of why it had been sent. The writer had been unable to sleep because of an inexplicable constraint on his spirit urging him to send money to the distant missionary couple. This experience was a milestone in C. T. Studd's life and decided a great deal of his future policy relating to the financial support of missions.[51]

We will close this chapter with a further illustration taken from missionary life. In 1910 James Outram Fraser (1886–1938) became the first missionary to the Lisu people of the upper Salween River valley in southwestern China. He was not much troubled by the primitive conditions and poor food that he had to endure, nor by the loneliness of his situation or the difficulties of visiting tribal settlements in a very mountainous area. What broke his heart was the spiritual hardness of the people and the fact that the few who professed faith soon fell back into their old ways.

Conscious that he was in a spiritual war, James made up his mind to give himself to steady, persistent prayer for the Lisu people. On 13th March 1916, this is what he wrote in his journal:

'After much pressure, even agony, in prayer for Lisu souls, enabled to break through into liberty, and to pray the definite prayer of faith for signal blessing among the Lisu during the next few months ... Real, prevailing prayer, for the first time for a week or more, and well worth the travail that led up to it … Much peace and rest of soul after making that definite prayer, and almost ecstatic joy to think of the Lisu Christian families I am going to get.'[52]

Fraser had previously set himself to get more and more prayer supporters to intercede for his work, while he himself not only prayed more, but tried to understand more about the life of prayer. In one of his letters home he had written about 'praying the prayer of definite faith':

'The very word "definite" means "with fixed limits." We are often exhorted, and with reason, to ask great things of God. Yet there is a balance in all things, and we may go too far in this direction. It is possible "to bite off," even in prayer, "more than we can chew." … There is no strain in the "rest of faith." It asks for definite blessings as God may lead. It does not hold back through carnal timidity, nor press ahead too far through carnal eagerness.

'I have definitely asked the Lord for several hundred families of Lisu believers. There are upwards of two thousand Lisu families in the Tantsah district. It might be said, "Why do you not ask for a thousand?" I answer quite frankly, "Because I have not faith for a thousand." I believe the Lord has given me faith for more than one hundred families, but not for a thousand. So I accept the limits the Lord has, I believe, given me.'[53]

In 1916, having spent the previous six years in faithful plodding as a travelling preacher, Fraser saw not only family after family, but village after village, making a public decision to turn from darkness to light, from the power of Satan to God. By 1918 over 600 Lisu people from 129 different families had been baptised, leading Fraser to write:

'I believe it was January 12, 1915, that I was definitely led to ask God for "several hundreds of families" from the Lisu. Some may say, "Your prayer has at last been answered." No! I took the answer *then*. I believed *then* that I had it. The realization has only now come, it is true, but God does not keep us waiting for *answers*. He gives them *at once*. Daniel 9:23.'[54]

The fruit of Fraser's missionary work remains to this day and the Lisu churches are stronger than ever. The assurance that he received in prayer has been more than realised. Speaking for myself, when I read of his experiences, I feel myself to be little more than an infant in the school of prayer. I am grateful for what I have learned so far, but long for more. There are whole continents of spiritual experience waiting for us to be explored! My prayer is that the Lord might be pleased to use this modest chapter to stir us up to seek a fuller and deeper understanding of what it means to ask and to receive.

7. Waiting on the Lord

*In our private communions with God, time is a
feature essential to its value. Much time spent
with God is the secret of all successful praying.*

E.M. BOUNDS[55]

From what we have said already it must be clear that
no Christian believer can have a life characterised by
holy emotions and balanced spiritual experience without
knowing something of what it means to wait on God. This
is especially true in the realms of guidance and of making
requests in prayer. Sadly, most preachers and churches today
do not have very much to say about this subject. That is why
we need this final chapter.

Waiting

Our modern world does not like waiting.[56] It puts no value on
it. In fact it detests it. Men and women express exasperation
if their queues do not move. Drivers sound their horns
at anyone who causes them the slightest delay and drum
their fingers impatiently when caught in a traffic jam. Office
workers groan with frustration when their computers slow

down. Children cry if their wishes are not granted right away. Speed is not enough. *Now* is what matters. 'Instant' is one of our culture's favourite words.

We should notice, however, that immediacy is not the only god before whom worldly people bow. They also worship the idol of activity. Busy people are looked up to, whatever may be the cause of their hustle. Elderly people are praised for remaining 'active', even if their activity is entirely self-centred. Being 'on the go' is everywhere regarded as a merit. There was a time when children were allowed to be bored, thus being forced to create their own amusement. This is no longer true. Now their every hour must be organised for them by well-meaning adults. The fact is that whoever you are, if you do not have 'something to do' you must expect to be misunderstood and criticised.

In complete contradiction to the impatience and busy-ness of this world, the Holy Scriptures call on us to 'wait on the Lord'. God's thoughts are not our thoughts. His ways are not our ways. He knows nothing of hurry. It is contrary to His nature. It follows that those who wish to know Him well must learn to walk at His speed. They must learn to slow down. In fact, they must come to a standstill, to stop, to be still and to wait. The God of the Bible is a Sabbath-creating God, and He calls on those who are made in His image to cherish a Sabbath day once a week, and to have many personal sabbath hours and moments in between. These 'mini-sabbaths' are times when we leave human company, find a place to be alone, close the door (either literally or metaphorically) and spend time in secret, waiting on our Father.[57]

In ordinary life, our times of waiting are of two sorts. There are those that are imposed on us and those that we choose. As a small child I remember an upstairs sash window coming down like a blunt guillotine and trapping my neck as I looked out. All I could do was to wait for rescue while a crowd of men below me laughed at my crying. That was not a moment that I chose. Nor did I choose to be stuck for two hours in a busy Mersey Tunnel, to wait in a dark lift during a power failure, or to lie for days in a hospital bed while other people investigated a medical problem I was having. On reflection I can see that each one of these waiting experiences had its own value. I learned that I was more dependent on other people than I had previously realised. I learned to appreciate my freedom of movement in a new way. As I resigned myself to each set of circumstances I eventually noticed that I was observing things with a closeness and scrutiny that I had seldom known before. But none of this was the result of my obeying any command to 'wait'.

There are other times, however, when we choose to wait, and we do this because we *care*. Walking with an elderly person, or with a small child, we wait for them because we care about their welfare. Unlike the down-and-out just sitting there for warmth and shelter, we wait for hours at the train station because we care about the person whom we are expecting to arrive. We wait through the night at the bedside of someone who is seriously ill because we care about them in a way that we cannot ever put into words. In situations like these we see the emptiness of our normal worldly instincts. 'Now' is no longer important. Speed does not matter. The last thing we want is to be 'on the go'. Something bigger is going through our minds, driven by the *care* we have for the person we are waiting for. Our waiting is the expression and the proof of our love.

It is the same with our waiting on God. We love Him so much that we will wait, and wait, and wait again, trusting that He, in His own time, will at last come and meet with us. It does not matter how long it takes. Our hope is in Him. Our expectation is from Him. So we stop everything and put ourselves in His presence. There we meditate on Him, worship Him and express our love for Him. We thank Him, confess our sins to Him, cry to Him on behalf of ourselves, and implore Him to meet the needs of others. We long and yearn and weep and sing and groan until, in the end, all we can do is to simply wait for Him in exhausted, blissful silence. Then at last—at long last!—He comes, and we know and feel Him to be near in all the ways we discovered in chapter 4.

When He comes

When he comes, wonderful things happen to us, both at that moment and in the long term. We enter into the experience that we explored in chapter 6—that of knowing that our prayers have been heard. Not only so, but we feel ourselves strengthened to bear the burdens that have been weighing us down. We are taken over by the conviction that we will be delivered in due time from the dangers we are facing. We find that we are more conscious than ever of how weak we are, yet we rise from our knees filled with courage to confront our enemies. We receive a clear view of the invisible, thus being enabled to walk our pilgrim way with a steadier tread. We feel that we are flying out of the reach of everything that would harm us. There is a new zest in us that we cannot define, but which removes from us all our previous thoughts of giving up the race or surrendering in the battle. In short, we prove that God's promise to us in Isaiah 40:28–31 is true:

'Have you not known? Have you not heard? The everlasting God, the LORD, the Creator of the ends of the earth, neither faints nor is weary. There is no searching of his understanding. He gives power to the weak, and to those who have no might he increases strength. Even the youths shall faint and be weary, and the young men shall utterly fall, but those who wait on the LORD shall renew their strength; they shall mount up with wings like eagles, they shall run and not be weary, they shall walk and not faint.'

'Waiting on the Lord' is not the same as simply spending a long time in prayer. It means communing with Him and pouring out our hearts to Him, until He touches our souls with the assurance that He has heard us. Every time of waiting is different from the previous occasion. The subjects that the Holy Spirit moves us to pray about, and the emotions that we feel, are as varied as those found in the 150 prayers of the Book of Psalms. The length of each time of prayer is similarly varied. What does not change is that whether we agonise in tears or bathe in joy, whether we confess our sins or pray against our enemies, whether we pray for ourselves or for Christ's church worldwide, our time apart is characterised by powerful, personal dealings between us and our God.

The Book of Psalms is the perfect textbook for all who want instruction in such waiting. It shows us that waiting on the Lord is the way to receive His guidance (25:5), to call down His protection (33:20), to know peace when surrounded by evil and when tempted to choose that path (37:7,9,34, 52:9), and to be sure of His rescue (40:1, 62:1–2). But it is not a quick business. It means watching and waiting for Him like those who watch and wait for the dawn (130:5–6).

Is it worth the wait? Oh yes! Those who deal with God in this way are never openly shamed and ruined by their enemies (25:3, 69:6). They are kept in the ways of integrity and uprightness (25:21), strengthened in their hearts (27:14), assured that wickedness will not ultimately prevail (37:34) and conquered by an overwhelming sense of the goodness of God (Lamentations 3:25–26). It is those who wait for Him who receive God's blessings in armfuls (Isaiah 30:18).

Quietness of soul

If we put together all the immediate blessings that we receive while waiting on God we may call them 'quietness of soul'. We do not hear much about this today. This is because many Christians do not experience it. It is not part and parcel of their daily lives. This being so, it is little wonder that so many of the Lord's people, particularly pastors and full-time Christian workers, are stressed, uptight, and finding it difficult to cope.

The yoke of Christ is easy. His burden is light (Matthew 11:30). His legacy to us is peace (John 14:27). It is His own peace that He gives us, and He does not give it sparingly. It is a peace which surpasses all understanding (Philippians 4:7). It is the privilege of every Christian to be able to face the worst scenario with an untroubled heart.

We enter into this peace by praying ourselves empty. This, supremely, is what happens as we wait on the Lord. Prayer, after all, is approaching God through Christ and telling Him everything we have on our heart at the moment. We go over it again and again until we have nothing left to say. We pour out our hearts until words fail us. We hold nothing back. We tell Him everything. When this has been done, further words simply seem out of place.

Real waiting on God usually ends in silence. In that silence, what peace invades the soul! With tear-stained cheeks we have confessed every sin we know about, and all our foolishness. What a sense of pardon we now have. We have told the Lord about every mistake, every worry, every fear, every ache and pain, every difficult decision. We have talked to Him about everyone we love, the sin of the world and the state of the churches. We have cast all our care on Him. We have thanked Him for every blessing we see. We have rejoiced in His being, His Word and His works. There is nothing to say which we have not said. We have prayed until we have fallen silent, and in that silence we wait.

It is then that He comes and bathes our hearts in a peace which we cannot define (Philippians 4:6–7). We feel the Father's embrace. We breathe the atmosphere of the Spirit. We find that Christ has never been so precious to us as now. It seems to us that we have everything—because we have *Him*.

The sustained silence that consummates real waiting on God is not the mere absence of words. The waves and billows have been stilled in our own heart. Something has happened inside us which will not leave us the moment we re-enter the busy, noisy, hurried, anxious world. We have quietness of soul and have been inwardly changed.

Long term effects

What starts in the secret place, then, is carried over into our daily life. Our waiting on the Lord has long term effects. Every hour of every day reveals the fact that the lives of those who regularly wait on God are radically different from those who don't. You can't have constant meetings with God and be the same as you were before.

Those who repeatedly wait on the Lord are quickly conquered by a conviction that burns itself into the depths of their soul and then dominates their thoughts and actions. Their strong, regular, personal dealings with God lead them to conclude *that there is only one Voice to listen to, only one Person to please.* This all-governing principle propels them into a life of simplicity.

For example, when they speak to others they are free from duplicity. They do not seek to curry favour. They do not hide the truth out of fear that it may offend someone, or that its disclosure may shut some doors of opportunity and work against their personal advancement. There is only one Person to please. This makes all their speech plain, honest and truthful. In addition, they are no longer consumed by the desire for recognition, status or position. Their security is not found in what they possess or which people of influence they know. They are delivered from the bondage of always trying to meet society's expectations. They can see through the lie that tells them that affluence leads to satisfaction. They are free, gloriously free—free from the desire for applause, free from all attempts to appear successful, free from trying to ensure that others have a good opinion of them—free to live for God *alone*.

Having come into this freedom through their long moments alone with God, those who wait on the Lord find that they have an increasing love of solitude. For them solitude is not loneliness. 'Loneliness is inner emptiness. Solitude is inner fulfilment.'[58] Just as you can be lonely in a crowd, you can also cultivate solitude while surrounded by people.[59] There, in your own spirit, you can withdraw and be alone with God and enjoy all the blessings that result. It goes without saying that the more often you have physically withdrawn from others in order to have dealings with Him, the easier such inward withdrawal becomes.

In this busy and over-populated world it is not easy to get away from people, and this is a subject to which we shall return. But those who know what it is to wait on the Lord have a constant desire to be alone with Him again, and so are always on the look out for opportunities to do so. They love His company, even if it often means waiting long hours for Him to come. So, while others seek to be with their friends, with all the banter, laughter, camaraderie, noise and shared experiences that this involves, God's friends search for and find 'little solitudes'[60] and secret places where they can be alone with Him.

Is not this being rather selfish and anti-social? Not at all. Those who are close to God know very well that He expects them to live with their feet on the ground in the real world. They are to treat every person they meet as a unique individual who has been made in God's image. They are to love them as they love themselves and are not to keep their distance from anybody. But they know that they cannot do this unless they are walking in intimate communion with their God. In their times alone with Him they see what a broken and sad world this is, and this fills them with compassion. They see that the deepest need of men and women is to be reconciled to God, and so they mingle amongst them with a sense of mission. They also find that by constantly putting themselves into God's presence, they are genuinely present when they are with others. They give them the whole of their attention. They desire nothing but their present and eternal welfare. And so they 'shine as lights in the world' (Philippians 2:15).

Silence

Besides loving solitude, those who wait on the Lord become lovers of silence. This is because solitude and silence go together, and our moments of waiting nearly always become silent before the Lord draws near and meets us. We are back, then, to the subject of how our private silences with God affect our day to day living. What are their long term effects?

In our secret silences we learn to *listen*. We turn the pages of the sacred Scriptures—pages we have coldly studied dozens of times—and hear the voice of the Good Shepherd with a clarity which astonishes us. We are awed, bow in worship and renew our vows of obedience. Normally no physical sound comes to our ears. But the Voice is unmistakeable and unforgettable. Should we ever hear it again, we know that we would recognise it straightaway, even if we did not have our Bible open at the time.

Yes, those who wait on the Lord become *listeners*, and this remains true when they are back in human company. When a thousand voices are clamouring for their attention and allegiance, there is only one Voice which really interests them. They are listening out for it all the time and they know that they will recognise it when it speaks. Counterfeit voices which claim to be the Eternal Voice they will reject.[61] *There is only one Voice to listen to*, and this is the voice that they must hear in all their decision making, as we saw in chapter 5.

Their ability to listen, however, also displays itself in the attention they give to those in need. Prayerful Christians know how to listen without interrupting. They do not feel the need to help people finish their sentences. They are prepared to let someone speak and speak, because they have learned long since how to wait without impatience. Such a capacity to listen is a rare jewel which is hardly ever found in worldly circles. It is one of the chief ways in which believers demonstrate how different they are from the unconverted. Simply listening to people is one of the surest ways to permanently help them. Once more we see that those who love God enough to withdraw from human company are in fact a great blessing to that company.

Our private silences have other long term effects. For example, we no longer feel the need of constant background music or other noises. And we speak less. We realise that most human speech is superfluous; the greater part of it is an exercise in self-justification. Silences in company no longer embarrass us. We engage in 'small talk' when it is helpful to the person in front of us but, overall, our words are fewer and fuller. We pause to reflect before we reply. Knowing what we can accomplish for them in the secret place, we feel no need to try and control others by our tongue, or to straighten them out. Our own souls have been changed by the silence of God and we instinctively know that people are not helped by torrents of words.

It is not only in unconverted company that we are different. Our experience of waiting on God has taught us a lot about our fellow believers. We have been brought to see that although our churches are populated by many active people, there are not among them many *deep* people. Any person, and any moment, can be deepened by silence. For example, when the Word has been preached, it needs to be thought about. Five minutes of meditative silence at the end of the service are worth far more than thirty minutes conversation on the church steps. It is in silence that the infallible Word percolates down into our souls.

And what an experience a walk in a park or the country now becomes! Only in unbroken silence can you hear the full music of God's creation. It ravishes the soul more than any human symphony. Unspeaking believers become attentive to the song of every bird and the sound of every insect. They hear distinct applause as the wind rustles the leaves of the branches and understand what it is for all the trees of the field to clap their hands (Isaiah 55:12). Their other senses, too, are sharpened. They see every colour as either more vivid or subtle. They learn to admire each species of flower and to feel the texture of each plant. God's world is scented with fragrances they never knew were there. 'The earth is full of the goodness of the Lord' (Psalm 33:5).

Walking with God

This brings us back, as promised, to the question of how a modern Christian can realistically get away from people in order to have a sustained opportunity to wait on the Lord. How in this twenty-first century can we obey our Lord's command to go into our room, to shut the door, and to pray to our Father who is in the secret place? (Matthew 6:6). After all, many of us live in crowded places and have busy lives which are subject to constant interruptions. Modern technology often seems to work against us, rather than for us. We do not feel that we have a moment's peace, let alone the chance to have an hour on our own.

All I can say is that my own life has been busier than most, but finding time to be alone has not been a significant problem. A simple discovery during my youth has shaped my life to this day. As I have mentioned in the Introduction, during my late teens our family moved from Chester to rural Pembrokeshire, where we eventually settled in the small village of Cosheston. What I did not tell you is that initially we lived in the even smaller village of Upper Nash. It was summer time when we arrived and in a couple of months I was to become a theological student. But what was I to do with myself during the weeks of waiting?

Apart from immediate family members, I knew nobody in the whole county. I found myself with no friends, no personal income, no transport and no town within reasonable walking distance. So I spent my mornings studying New Testament Greek and my afternoons walking in the countryside. And, as I walked, I found myself praying.

There was no one around, so I could pray out loud—very loudly if I wanted to! I have to confess that I was very much a babe in prayer in those days. My prayers were mostly composed of requests, and dominant among them was the plea that the Lord would make me useful in His cause. There was very little in the way of worship, of thanksgiving, or of confession of sin. But I had learned the lesson that I was never to forget: *it is easy to pray in an unhurried way out of doors.*

I trust that my prayer life today is more mature than it was then, but outside is where most of my praying still gets done. It keeps me from giving in to the temptation to start other work before having a time of sustained communion with God. Despite what some people say, it is just as easy to pray in the inner city as it is the countryside, as thirty-five years of pastoral ministry there have proved to me. Adoration, thanksgiving, detailed confession of sin, intercession, petition and renewed dedication can take place on a pavement just as well as they can on a rural path. I know what it is to stand in awe at a felt sense of the presence of God both in the silence of the fields and when jostled by pedestrians on a busy street with its buses, taxis, lorries and smoke. Of both it can be said, 'How awesome is this place! This is none other than the house of God, and this is the gate of heaven!' (Genesis 28:17).[62]

Whether in city or country, I still find it easier to pray out loud—although shouting and singing are probably better reserved for lonelier places, parks and buildings! In cities and towns I find that the faces of the people, with their hurry and bustle, instead of being a distraction, serve rather as a stimulus to pray. And inevitably, whatever the context, I find that the longer I wait on God the more likely it is that I will fall into silence, when 'only my heart's desire cries out in me'.[63] This silence is not made any the less profound by the fact that British weather often obliges me to pray in warm, waterproof clothes and under a large umbrella!

The point is that holy emotions and spiritual experiences are matters of the *heart* and not of geography. It is the heart that matters. It is the spiritual health of the heart that, above all, needs to be cultivated. 'Above all else, guard your heart, for it is the wellspring of life' (Proverbs 4:23).[64] If this modest book has helped its readers to see the importance of this, and has helped them to begin doing it, it has more than served its purpose.

Endnotes

1. These two lines are from Joseph Hart's hymn, 'Let us ask the important question'. It is no. 237 in *A Selection of Hymns for Public Worship* by William Gadsby (London: The Gospel Standard Publications, 1961).

2. The word 'unction' comes from the French word *onction*, which means 'anointing'. Anointed preaching has the characteristics that I have used in describing Hywel Griffiths' ministry.

3. This is a quotation from *Daniel Rowland and the Great Evangelical Awakening in Wales* by Eifion Evans (Edinburgh, The Banner of Truth Trust, 1985), p.378. In the section where this line is found Dr Evans is summarising the root convictions of the great Welsh preacher.

4. This expression was first used by John Wesley to describe part of his conversion experience at a meeting held in Aldersgate Street, London, on Wednesday, 24th May, 1738.

5. See John Bunyan, *Grace Abounding to The Chief of Sinners*, chapter 10. Written by Bunyan in 1665, while he was imprisoned in Bedford Jail, this book has been through countless editions since it was published in 1666.

6. I am writing this chapter from notes that I made years ago. Although I have studied the Bible on this subject, I am more than aware that what follows is heavily dependent on the insights of others. My problem is that I can't always remember who I was reading at the time. But I do know that I am regurgitating a good deal of *A Treatise Concerning Religious Affections* by Jonathan Edwards (1703–58) (Ed. by John E. Smith, New Haven: Yale University Press, 1959) and that I owe a lot to John Murray in *Collected Writings of John Murray*,

Volume 2, Chapter 3 (Edinburgh: The Banner of Truth Trust, 1977, reprinted 2009). How I thank the Risen Lord for the great teachers that He has given to His church throughout the centuries!

7. See *The Institutes of the Christian Religion* 1:15:7.

8. This phrase is taken from Charles Wesley's well known hymn, 'Love divine, all loves excelling'. It is no. 653 in *Christian Hymns* (Bridgend, Evangelical Movement of Wales, 2007).

9. Augustine (354–430), Bishop of Hippo in North Africa, lived through the time when the Roman Empire was disintegrating. Converted from a grossly immoral and unbelieving life, he became one of the greatest preachers and writers in the whole of Christian history.

10. Martin Luther (1483–1546) dismantled the monopoly of the Roman Catholic Church by insisting that our only authority in deciding what we believe and practise should be the Holy Scriptures.

11. Most of what now follows has been previously published in *The Banner of Truth* magazine, Issue 555 (Edinburgh: The Banner of Truth Trust, 2009).

12. The Holy Spirit clearly did this in the case of John the Baptist, who was regenerate before he was born, and cannot possibly have been regenerated through contact with the Word. See Luke 1:15. Later on we find the unborn John thrilled at being in the presence of the unborn Saviour and His mother. See Luke 1:39–45. The Spirit was clearly at work in John, without the Word.

13. The same is true of Romans 10:17. Faith is exercised at the moment when the new life becomes visible, not at the moment of germination. Others have quoted Hebrews 4:12 in favour of the Lutheran position. But this is neither a reference to the germination of new life nor to its becoming visible. The apostle is writing to those who need to question whether they are truly on the road to heaven. The way for them to find out is to expose themselves to the Word of God, which will search them out, destroying false assurance and confirming true assurance.

14. *The Westminster Confession of Faith*, drawn up in 1647, was ratified and established by Acts of Parliament in 1649 and 1690. This extract is from chapter 18, paragraph 1.

15. A great deal of the content of this chapter has already appeared in my *You Might have Asked* (Welwyn: Evangelical Press, 1983) chapter 11. With his permission, that chapter leaned heavily on two articles by Donald MacLeod in *The Banner of Truth* magazines of October and November 1974.

16. See Romans 4:5.

17. D. Martyn Lloyd-Jones, *Authority* (London: Inter-Varsity Fellowship, 1962), p.78.

18. See 2 Corinthians 1:22 and Ephesians 1:13–14.

19. In this extract R.B. Jones is writing about the Welsh Revival, and in particular the extraordinary events of November 1904, in which he was involved personally. See R.B. Jones, *Rent Heavens* (London: Pioneer Mission, 1948) p.41.

20. *Collins Plain English Dictionary* (London: Harper Collins Publishers, 1996), p.495.

21. Those who are unclear about this most basic Bible truth of all should read my brief book *What the Bible teaches about the Trinity* (Darlington: EP Books, 2011). The three paragraphs now following are adapted extracts from this book.

22. Those who are new to this subject might be pleased to read my book *Jesus is both God and Man* (Darlington, Evangelical Press, 2000), where I deal with theophanies in chapter 4, 'The promise of a man' (pp.77–87).

23. Here I quote the Revised Standard Version of the Bible because, at this point, I believe it catches the sense more satisfactorily. See *The Holy Bible: Revised Standard Version* (London: Thomas Nelson and Sons Ltd, 1957), p.950.

24. This is an expression used by A.W. Tozer and is the title of chapter 5 in his wonderful book *The Pursuit of God* (London: Marshall, Morgan and Scott, 1961) p.61.

25. The dates are correct, although the Revival is often referred to as the '1904–05' revival. There is no doubt that this extraordinary work of the Spirit began in 1903.

26. *Rent Heavens*, p.41.

27. The quotation is from James Packer's article 'Thou our Guide' in *The Evangelical Magazine*, no. 47, September 1967, p.5.

28. For example, see Romans 14:1–15:13 and 1 Corinthians chapter 9.

29. I read this quotation from Dr G. Campbell Morgan years ago and wrote it down, but I no longer remember where it is found. If I find out, I will include the reference in any subsequent editions of this book.

30. He uses the expression in the article quoted above, p.6.

31. The quotation is from the Authorised (King James) Version of the Bible, which the church was using at the time.

32. Howell Harris (1714–1773) was one of the principal preachers in the great awakening that swept through Wales in the eighteenth century. He, George Whitefield, Daniel Rowland and William Williams were the founding fathers of the Calvinistic Methodist Connexion which, until quite recently, was the largest Christian body in the Principality.

33. This extract is from Richard Bennett, *The Early Life of Howell Harris* (London: The Banner of Truth Trust, 1962), p.27. The biblical quotation is from Malachi 3:6.

34. Bennett, p.24.

35. Bennett, p.42.

36. These events are recounted by Arnold Dallimore, *Spurgeon, A New Biography* (Edinburgh: The Banner of Truth Trust, 1985), pages 38 and 46.

37. See Acts 16:6–15.

38. See Jeremiah 45:5.

39. This incident is narrated by Dr D. Eryl Davies in John Emyr (ed), *A Father in the Faith* (Bridgend: Bryntirion Press, 2012), pp.17–18.

40. A very good place to start would be to read Jim Thompson, *Prophecy today* (Darlington: Evangelical Press, 2008).

41. Matthew 6:10,

42. *The Westminster Shorter Catechism*, Answer 102.

43. See Acts 6:4.

44. Romans 8:26.

45. See John Emyr (Ed), *A Father in the Faith* (Bridgend: Bryntirion Press, 2012), p.160. Mr. Davies' article 'Believe that ye receive', which is the final chapter of the book, is one of the most helpful pieces ever written about our subject. More than a few echoes of this article are to be found in my treatment here.

46. D.M. M'Intyre, *The Hidden Life of Prayer* (Minneapolis: Bethany Fellowship, 1978), pp.87–88 . Some of us believe that this book is one of the greatest books on prayer ever written.

47. Quoted by D.M. M'Intyre, *op. cit.*, pp.88–89. Toplady is best known for his famous hymn, 'Rock of ages, cleft for me'.

48. Quoted by D.M. M'Intyre, *op. cit.*, p.89.

49. These three expressions are used by Elwyn Davies in the article referred to above, p.158.

50. This incident is narrated in detail in Norman Grubb, *C.T. Studd* (London: The Religious Tract Society, 1934), pp.98–99.

51. C.T. Studd (1860–1931) was a famous English cricketer and one of 'The Cambridge Seven' who sailed as missionaries to China in 1885. He spent his life in missionary work in China, India and Africa, and founded what is now know as the Worldwide Evangelisation Crusade (WEC), one of whose principles is that no appeals should ever be made for financial support.

52. J.O. Fraser, *The Prayer of Faith* (London: China Inland Mission, undated), p.7.

53. J.O. Fraser, p.19.

54. J.O. Fraser, pp.26–27.

55. E.M. Bounds, *Power through Prayer* (Grand Rapids: Clarion Classics, Zondervan Publishing House, not dated), p.35.

56. A book which has stimulated me to think about the subject of waiting, and which is no doubt echoed in some parts of this chapter, is W.H. Vanstone, *The Stature of Waiting* (London: Darton, Longman and Todd Ltd, 1982), especially its final chapter.

57. See Matthew 6:6.

58. This helpful quotation is from Richard Foster, *Celebration of Discipline* (London: Hodder and Stoughton, 1989), p.121. Those who would like to know more about Simplicity and Solitude would do well to read Foster's chapters on these subjects.

59. This is clear from Luke 9:18, which in the NIV helpfully reads, 'Once when Jesus was praying in private and his disciples were with him ...'

60. The expression is Richard Foster's, Ibid. p.131.

61. See John 10:4–6 and 1 John 2:18–20.

62. In a recent e-mail a friend said to me, 'I want to say thank you for something really helpful that I believe you told *.*. and that he passed on to me: going for walks to pray every day. While I have always known its importance I have struggled with actually doing this area of pastoral work, but walking has revolutionised (no exaggeration) my prayer life. Our trainee pastor *.*. has also been doing this and is finding it very helpful.'

63. This phrase is taken from the second verse of the hymn 'None other Lamb, none other Name' by Christina Georgina Rossetti (1830–94). It is no. 581 in *Christian Hymns* (Bridgend: Evangelical Movement of Wales, 2004).

64. The quotation is from the New International Version (NIV).